COMPANY COMING
SIX DECADES OF HOSPITALITY

by Ruth Stout

Author of *Gardening Without Work*

Norton Creek Press
http://www.nortoncreekpress.com

Company Coming
Six Decades of Hospitality

by Ruth Stout

ISBN 978-0-9819284-8-7

Originally published by 1958 by Exposition Press.

Norton Creek Press
36475 Norton Creek Rd.
Blodgett OR 97326
http://www.nortoncreekpress.com

For my sisters

JUANITA AND MARY

ELIZABETH AND MAY

CONTENTS

I We Didn't Call Them Guests 11

II Wash Day—An Old Bicycle—Melodrama 18

III Carrie Nation—More Drama—The Hammock Scene 27

IV A Distinguished Guest for Tea—Dinner Served in
    Courses 35

V Guests Seem to Multiply 39

VI Greenwich Village—A Hypnotist—Russia 48

VII Poverty Hollow and Here They Come! 62

VIII Fish Out of Water 74

IX God Blesses Our Home But He Doesn't Sweep It 86

X Pre-Sputnik Sputnik 93

XI The Bank Fails 100

XII A War Casualty 111

XIII Everyone Loves Dogs and Children—Yeah? 123

XIV Some Famous People—Mrs. John Doe 132

XV It's a Gift 140

XVI This I Believe 149

COMPANY COMING

CHAPTER I

We Didn't Call Them Guests

ON THAT SOMEWHAT HAPHAZARD FARM in Wakarusa, Kansas (the first home that I remember), visitors were probably the one thing we never ran short of. We didn't call them guests; they were just friends who came to see us for an afternoon, overnight, a week, a month.

That was more than sixty years ago. We often came across house parties and house guests in novels (which ranged in quality from The Duchess to Henry James), and such goings-on seemed excitingly sophisticated and unattainable. However, we were optimistic youngsters and felt that some day we would no doubt see some of these fascinating creatures, and possibly even have one in our own home. We didn't realize we were already somewhat oversupplied with them.

I can't figure out how on earth Dad managed to feed all of them. He was County Superintendent of Schools, with whatever salary they paid in those days; it couldn't have been enough to have had much left to throw about, what with eight children to bring up. (The youngest, Donald, wasn't born yet.) But, at least, that was before the days when parents began to worry about a college education for their child before it was conceived.

Each week when we drove to Sunday School there was never any telling how many of our friends would pile into our spring-wagon to go home with us for Sunday dinner. If Dad was concerned about all the food they were going to consume, he never let on.

Mother took this the way she took everything: philosophically. She didn't scramble around for more food, she put us to scrambling: "Juanita, wash eight more potatoes; Rex, better run out and pick two quarts of peas; Ruth, when you set the table, don't forget the five extra places."

For unexpected guests in summer, we picked extra beans, corn, peas, tomatoes. For dessert, strawberries in spring, muskmelon or watermelon a little later, peaches and grapes.

In winter it was even simpler; the menu was seldom elaborate but *plenty* was the watchword. The Stout National Dish, which was navy beans and a hunk of salt pork simmered together gently for hours, was everybody's favorite. Our family all still love it, whether gastronomically or nostalgically, I couldn't say.

I still remember how surprised, even almost horrified I was, many years ago, when, visiting various friends, I saw how their mothers waited on them. I stayed all night with a German girl once; there were two grown girls and a boy of sixteen in the family, yet it was the mother who hurried down to the corner bakery to get fresh rolls for breakfast. And there was an Italian girl who invited a few of us for dinner one Sunday; her mother waited on everyone, didn't even sit down at the table with us. I was awfully embarrassed.

I mention the nationality in these cases because we had lived in New York only about six months, and I thought it must have something to do with European customs.

This was years before the present era of Infantriarchal Society. I am no longer ever surprised at the things parents do for, and take from, their children and am only occasionally shocked.

In those far-off days in Wakarusa we hadn't heard about Hospitality with a capital H. We hadn't heard that a guest could do no wrong, that your house belonged to him while he was in it, that however difficult and unpalatable it might be for you, he had to be treated with courtesy. Therefore, with no such high standards to hamper us, it isn't surprising that our guests didn't always get first-class treatment.

There was, for instance, Mrs. Ross, the wife of some Important Person, a Lady Who Had A Maid, who called on Mother one day. This was the real thing: a formal call, rare in our experience. But we weren't impressed; we didn't know that the wife of the Superintendent of Schools was a person one called on, while our dearest friends' mothers, mere farmers' wives and poor ones at that, were not. If we had known that Mrs. Ross had never called on our nearest neighbor, Mrs. Whipple, we would have assumed she just hadn't got around to it yet.

As a matter of fact we were pretty well grown up before we knew there were such odd things in the world as lower, middle, and upper classes. I think this must have been because we had, in our environment, close friends in all three strata. The lords, ladies, millionaires, and other snobs in the novels we read were to us, I think, like the princes in fairy tales—enchanting, but unreal.

Back to the caller, Mrs. Ross: she arrived in all her finery, and sat down on a piece of sticky flypaper, which (one wonders why) was temporarily lying on our best chair. The boys, not having learned that any mishap short of fire should be treated as if it didn't exist if there was a guest present, roared with laughter; it was funny to them, and when something is funny, you laugh.

When May, the oldest of us, began to have beaux, the various young men who came to see her didn't fare very well if Rob and Walt (two and four years younger than May) didn't think they measured up. Sometimes the boys would hide the suitor's overcoat, sometimes they would slip salt into his dish of strawberries. If they had nothing more interesting to do, they enjoyed sneaking out and taking a long ride in the young man's buggy, particularly if they knew he was planning to take May driving that evening. One of their favorite tricks was to swipe, from the caller's coat pocket, the box of candy he had brought to give to May, and pass the candy around, apologizing for its poor quality.

Mother had her own system of treating those of May's beaux whom she didn't care for much, although of course none of us realized her motive at the time. She would invite the undesirables to our home so frequently that they always seemed to be underfoot, and in no time at all May was ready for a change.

The most exciting guests were the young ladies from Topeka (ten miles away) who would stay overnight with May when there was a party in Wakarusa. It is surprising, as I think of them now, that they all seemed so beautiful, but it could be that to a romantic ten-year-old any young lady of eighteen is glamorous if she has a beau.

When the parties were at our house they were, for me, a maddening conglomeration of glorious excitement and agony. The first two hours were like a novel, with all the girls so coquettish and gay and the young men so dashing and witty. It was a mere nothing that Juanita, two years older than I, was at least a dozen times as pretty, for, thanks to curling kids, my hair was in soft gold ringlets and my dress (usually somebody's old one made over) was always by far the prettiest I had ever owned. I was sure that one of those Romeos (preferably Roy Nelson or Jonas Snyder) would remind himself that beauty was only skin deep and then it would be but a few minutes before he discovered the lofty aims and fine ideals hiding behind my freckles.

But before that had time to happen, always came the disaster: I grew painfully, agonizingly sleepy. I looked enviously at Juanita; her blue eyes were as bright and wide open as could be. And Rex, still under ten but with more will power than any one person has a right to, looked as if it were nine o'clock in the morning. My eyelids grew heavier and heavier until finally I gave up; it was no use. Oh no, I didn't go to bed; I curled up in a big chair and was soon deep in dreamland.

I have always felt that falling asleep belongs near the top of the list of pleasurable sensations. If the day has been difficult and you have reason to expect a similar one tomorrow, what a wonderful feeling to know that you can escape for a while! And if you've had a pleasant day, with the prospect of the next one being the same, falling asleep between the two is like drifting lazily in a canoe from one enchanting land to another.

During those few seconds as we pass into unconsciousness we are happy and good, uncritical, without greed or hate or envy or hypocrisy or worry. It is true that this looks a bit negative on paper; we aren't hating but neither are we loving. I'm not going to erase it, however, for I want to pay my small tribute to that gentle little trip into unconsciousness.

During those Wakarusa years our Christmas guests were always the same: the Overmyers. They lived in Bellevue, a suburb of Topeka, and when we didn't go to their home for Christmas, they came to ours. Dad and Mr. Overmyer had gone to school together; they were like brothers.

I wonder which Mother preferred: getting dinner for six Overmyers and twelve of us (Grandma and Grandpa Stout lived in a small house on our farm), or piling the lot of us into the spring-wagon, riding the thirteen miles to Bellevue behind Dan and Old Beck, and home again at night. Then the worst part: the job of getting a flock of tired children into bed.

When we reached home, in the cold and the dark, Dad would build a fire, while Rob and Walt lit the kerosene lamps. Mother and May were busy with the little ones, Mary and Elizabeth. Juanita and Rex lent a hand here and there.

But I was a shivery child and as I remember it all I did was stand in misery as close to the stove as possible, cold in body, defeated in spirit, vowing never to get married, and if I did, not to have any cold, sleepy, cross children. Or if I did have children, *never* to take them out of a nice warm house.

Another thing against going away on Christmas Day: who wants to get presents and then go off and leave them all day long? Of course you could wear your new hair ribbon and take your chief present if it was a doll, but not if it was a set of dishes or a doll cradle. If you went off and left your gifts, having had them so short a time, you couldn't be absolutely sure whether you actually owned them or whether it was just another one of your unattainable dreams. And no matter how many books you got, there was no use taking even one with you; just try to take the tiniest little peek into it!

So it was better for me when it was the Overmyers' turn to be the guests, and probably no greater burden to Mother, since everybody helped. Grandma made mince pies, with her own mincemeat, and the things which are called by that name nowadays couldn't claim to be even a tenth cousin to those pies of hers. And May was not only an efficient worker but an able organizer as well; she could organize Juanita and me into helping cheerfully even on Christmas Day.

On these occasions Mrs. Overmyer never failed to offer me her son George (nine years older than I was) for my husband, as a reward for some job I did. I never knew why she picked me, but it must have been because Juanita was so much more efficient than I. Mrs. Overmyer probably didn't realize that Mother and May often took pains to give me the appreciation I didn't earn; I sort of dreamed my way through the days, and am afraid I seldom deserved any praise for a job well done.

Mrs. Overmyer was very kind and probably thought I was envious of Juanita's superior gifts but it happened that she was mistaken. I was a resourceful and imaginative child, and having noticed that I wasn't pretty or capable, I settled for nobility of soul; you didn't have to be born with that, you could achieve it.

Who wanted to be beautiful, anyway, since it was only skin deep? As for Juanita's talent for sewing, why on earth should anyone want to sew? She could cook, too, while I burned everything. Well, of course, nobody prefers to ruin the dinner, but she was, after all, two years older than I; a couple more years and I would no doubt be able to keep my mind on the boiling pot.

Juanita had certainly never written a lovely poem, with ten verses, which swung along like a song, every verse ending with "On Narragansett Bay." The bay had nothing to do with the rest of the poem but those words made such a nice sing-song end to each verse! I was too smart to let anyone older than

Juanita read it; I knew that old people would be likely to offer advice, and I didn't want advice—only admiration.

Mrs. Overmyer couldn't know that I wasn't envious of Juanita, since it was obvious that I had plenty of reason to be, so that must have been why she offered George to me. I was too timid to tell her that George looked more like the villain, to me, than the hero of a romance. He was quite dark, very handsome, and lacked only a little mustache to play the part of the villain in any novel I had so far read.

If I had been the heroine of a novel, I'd have known at first glance that George was the villain, and thus have saved myself from abduction, which was what happened to heroines in those days. However, this would have spoiled the story; to make it fill a whole book, the heroine had to be definitely on the stupid side, otherwise, how could the villain possibly have kept her in such hot water up to the very last few pages?

CHAPTER II

Wash Day—An Old Bicycle—Melodrama

DONALD WAS BORN six years after Elizabeth and was only a month old when we moved to Bellevue, a few minutes' walk from the Overmyers. Dad sold the farm which I'm sure was heavily mortgaged, and the sale included Grandpa's house, so he and Grandma went along with us.

The man who bought the farm had come on a Sunday and stayed for dinner. We children didn't know what was going on but something happened which made it obvious that it was big enough to change our whole lives. It was a hot day, and in the distance we heard the tinkling bell of the ice-cream wagon which didn't pass by our farm more than a few times all summer long; we all made a mad dash for our banks, and also, feeling it was only fair, we sent Elizabeth to ask Dad to contribute a nickel. He gave her a quarter instead and mentioned it, so we knew it wasn't a mistake; we began to figure that this man had come to tell Dad about a long-lost rich uncle who had died and left us a fortune.

When we found out the farm was sold, we shed some quiet tears. It is a sad thing to go far away from your friends, and in those days thirteen miles was very far—a sad thing to turn your back on the little white schoolhouse, on our haystack, the big walnut and cottonwood trees, the brook, the cozy little outhouse, the lilac hedge, cherry and apple orchards, strawberry patch, wild verbenas and daffodils. We had to say good-by to the horses, Dan and Molly (dear Old Beck had died), for there was neither room nor need for horses on our new little patch of ground. Rumor, the cat, and Sir Philip Bruce-Errington, the dog, went with us, of course.

May was teaching school about seven miles from Bellevue, and she boarded near the school, but came home for Saturday and Sunday. Rob and Walt opened a feed store in Topeka; they had to walk only about a mile to get the streetcar into town.

The rest of us went to the Bellevue School. Juanita and I were ready for high school, but in those horse-and-buggy days I suppose it would have been too complicated to get us to Topeka every day. Streetcars weren't very obliging; their schedule would have landed us at school either too early or too late.

The stream of guests soon began to flow again; we each acquired a new chum along with an ample supply of lesser friends.

Juanita began to have beaux. May told me that if I wouldn't go with a boy until I was sixteen, she would buy me a pair of red kid gloves, and since there was nothing in the world I wanted as much, I told her I would try to earn them. Also, there was no one in sight, just then, whom I wanted to go with, and I somehow didn't expect the Prince to turn up in Bellevue; it wasn't a suitable setting. Besides, what on earth did a girl talk about to her beau?

May's and Juanita's suitors seldom stayed more than a few minutes, just long enough for the girls to get their wraps. Then they were off, for a buggy ride, or to a party, or something. My guess is that it was often *something*—that they stopped the buggy and did a little spooning, which later was called necking (and by now I hope they have a prettier word for it). I remember I didn't feel exactly critical of this, just pleasantly melancholy —sorry for the future husband, cheated out of an unkissed bride.

Art Hawkes was not only one of Juanita's most devoted admirers but was also Walt's best friend. In one or the other of these roles, he practically lived at our house and on washday he was our biggest asset.

In summer, doing the washing was as much fun as a party, or rather, it *was* a party. We filled our old washing machine with hot, soapy water, dumped some clothes into it, then two people, one on each side, took hold of the two handles and rocked the machine to and fro. In nice weather we always did the washing in the backyard and eight or ten of our friends would come to help so that we would be ready to play sooner.

Art always came to these affairs but not as a helper. He was an aristocrat, the only one of us who had an allowance, and he paid his way by bringing bananas and cookies, so it was only fair that he shouldn't help. Being profoundly in love with him, I was glad he didn't do any work; he was too grownup, anyway, to do anything as unimportant as washing clothes. It was much more fitting that he should just lean against a tree and joke and hand out bananas.

In the wintertime Mrs. Whitestone did our washing, and since she ate lunch with us, I count her a guest. As a matter of fact my conception of a guest is elastic; it seems to include everyone to whom I open the door and say "Come in," from an invited friend to the mendacious male who is selling magazines to put himself through college. Which reminds me: to make short work, once, of one of those who said he was going to be a doctor, I lied, too; I said I was a Christian Scientist and didn't believe in doctors. He suddenly decided to study law instead of medicine, but I fooled him; I suddenly decided I had no use for lawyers, either.

Back to Mrs. Whitestone: I'm sorry to say it, but hers was a family you would really have to call low-grade in several respects. They were all almost repulsively unattractive, had no sense of humor whatever, were pitifully short on intelligence, and there was no special indication that a single one of them even had the heart of gold which is such a handy thing to say about a person who has nothing else to offer.

They were the sort of people about whom Mother would say: "They do the best they can," which she fell back on when she couldn't think of a single specific virtue. When Walt went to Colorado, looking for adventure and a job, and got desperately homesick, he wrote to Mother: "I'd even be glad to see the Whitestones."

James Whitestone, who was two years older than I, was

in Rex's class at the Bellevue school; James had a dreadful time with his lessons. Mother told his mother that perhaps one of us children could help him, and I was somehow chosen for the job. He came several afternoons a week after school, for an hour, and I would struggle with him while the voices of Elizabeth and Rex and Mary and some of our friends floated in from the yard or from another room.

I aimed too high, for I didn't realize that the poor boy simply didn't have it in him. I wasn't satisfied when, teaching him reading, I finally got him to take a breath after a period, but tried to have him make another, shorter pause after commas. Much more than that, I wanted him to sound as though he understood what it was all about. When he would finally get through a sentence without a mistake, we would go back and work on expression, often laboring with one sentence for the whole hour.

I think Mother finally noticed how exhausted and desperate both James and I looked after these lessons, for she somehow put a stop to them.

After I sprained my ankle at a picnic, everyone who came to the house was so attentive to me that it made me feel quite important. Each one seemed to be my personal guest.

I was afraid to even try to put my weight on my foot, and used crutches for weeks. I enjoyed this to some extent but I guess Mother didn't, for when she heard of a colored woman who cured people by massage, she asked her to come and look at my ankle. The woman came at once; she was big and black and she had about the kindest, cheeriest, most reliable face I had ever seen. Everybody called her Aunt Lucindy.

She gazed at my foot (which hadn't been swollen for quite a while), gave it a few brisk rubs and pinches, then smiled and said: "Now you can walk, child."

I got right up and walked and it didn't hurt a bit, and quite naturally I put it down as a miracle, ignoring the comments of a few people to the effect that my ankle had been all right

for ages and that I was just a coward. I knew I was a coward
about pain but it didn't concern me, for I couldn't see any
particular reason for a girl to be physically brave; that was
for boys. On the other hand, I had every intention to be morally
and spiritually courageous, even to the point of death if the
occasion should require it; provided I wasn't tortured, of course.

Aunt Lucindy stayed to dinner that night, and often came
to see us after that. She stands out in my memory as one of
the most enjoyable guests we have ever had.

I thought up one rather unique way to entertain girls who
stayed all night with Juanita and me; we shared a room with
two beds in it and these were large enough for us to have two
all-night guests at once. I was always the first to get into bed,
skipping such unnecessary things as brushing my hair and
washing my face and was usually asleep by the time the others
got these little jobs done.

One night Juanita and I, after a party, brought our chums,
Minnie Stewart and Ethel Chapman, home with us to spend the
night. At that time all four of us were crazy about Otis Vail,
who was engaged to marry some older girl, and after I hopped
into bed I got to thinking about him and this kept me wide-
awake. When the lamp was finally turned out and everything
was quiet, I still couldn't get to sleep and decided to have
some fun out of it; I thought up the idea of pretending to be
talking in my sleep. I began to mumble some things about Otis,
and the other girls were simply fascinated.

In the morning they could hardly wait to tell me what I
had said, but they left out the two best things, and it was all
I could do to keep still about them. After that, I gave several
such performances, but once I said something which made me
burst out laughing and that was of course the end of that form
of entertainment.

Rob now rode to the feed store on a bicycle, a secondhand
one and quite a wreck; after a while he bought a new one and

gave the wreck to us children. Rex and I became expert riders and if he wasn't on it, I was. Donald and Elizabeth were too little to attempt it; Mary couldn't even reach the pedals from the seat, she rode standing up on them. Juanita was too sophisticated now to bother.

This was the only bicycle in Bellevue available to youngsters, and after school anywhere from fifteen to twenty-five of our playmates would go home with us for a ride. With so many, there was no time to spare for giving lessons; they stood in line waiting for a ride on the handlebars, Rex and I taking turns giving each one a spin down the road.

Every now and then we let Mary have a chance, and at her insistence tried putting the smallest child on the handlebars. Off they went, Mary standing up on the pedals. Before long, she was giving rides to children twice her size.

I suppose there must have been quite a few accidents, but none were fatal—surely I would remember if anyone had been killed.

One of the many reasons why we loved to have Amy Overmyer come to see May was because she never failed to ask us to "have scenes." This started in the Wakarusa days, when a small troupe of actors, consisting of Mr. and Mrs. Powell and their little daughter, gave an evening's entertainment in our schoolhouse. I'm sure they must have been regrettably short on talent. And now, when I close my eyes and recall her, I think Mrs. Powell's face was probably emaciated from worry and insufficient food rather than thrillingly haggard from her tragic role, as it seemed to us then.

Never having seen anyone "act" before, the Powells took our breath away with what seemed to us their wit and glamor, and needless to say, we rushed home and began to "have scenes."

At first we meticulously repeated the Powells' performance, but soon we looked down on their feeble plot and began to make up our own, usually thinking them up in advance. Sometimes, however, when the grownups clamored for an act and we had nothing prepared, we would just decide what each actor was to be—hero or villain, heroine or villainess—and make up the story as we went along.

In Bellevue now, living near the Overmyers, we added Grace and David to the cast, wrote longer plays, learned lines, rehearsed, set a night for the performance and charged a penny admission. I could probably fill a volume with stories of these plays but this isn't a book about the drama; I'll tell about only one.

For this particularly complicated melodrama, we were short of actors. In a breathlessly tense scene—the hero at the altar, about to marry the villainess, who had intercepted letters to him from the sweet but not very bright heroine (this dastardly thing seemed to be known by everyone except the hero)—the poor fellow cries out: "Why am I just learning of this? Why did no one tell me?" We needed someone to reply: "*I* wrote to you."

So we gave that one line to little Dorothy Graves, who lived next door to us (for some reason which I can't remember no other actor in the cast could say it) and at rehearsal she learned to speak promptly on cue, but instead of saying "*I* wrote to you" she would say "I wrote to *you*."

Now the audience would most certainly not have noticed this, and if they had, would have overlooked it, since Dorothy was only about five years old, but with our high standards, the smallest flaw wasn't permissible.

A thousand times, I'm sure, we corrected her, saying over and over "*I* wrote to you" and beating our breasts to emphasize the "I," but she couldn't do it; she just didn't see the difference. She would obligingly, frantically, beat her breast when saying the words, but the accent stayed on "you."

Finally, when we were all exhausted, one of us suddenly pointed out that the line was entirely unnecessary, added nothing, wouldn't be missed, so we told Dorothy we had decided to take it out. The tears began to roll down her cheeks; there was nothing to do but let her ruin the play.

A miracle happened: the night of the play, when the hero cried out his reproach, Dorothy came through, right on cue. "*I wrote to you*," she said, and the other actors were so astonished that they all but wrecked the big scene.

Just before we moved to Topeka our school gave an oyster supper. Each table, seating eight, had a boy and a girl to serve it, and my co-worker happened to be Vern Byers. All this was satisfactory except for one embarrassing feature: the boy who waited on table with a girl was supposed to take her home.

A double dilemma: I could talk to jolly Vern at recess or at a party or when he came to see Walt (they were great pals), but what on earth did you talk about to a boy who was seeing you home? Much more important, there was the matter of the red kid gloves May was going to buy for me if I didn't go with a boy until I was sixteen. Even if I had been a little attracted to Vern, which certainly wasn't the case, one short walk home would hardly be worth the sacrifice of those gloves.

I kept my great problem to myself, not even telling Juanita, although I can't imagine why; she probably could have solved it in some slick way, since she knew all about that aspect of life and its intricacies.

The night arrived; the serving was fun, and the oyster stew was so good that I enjoyed it in spite of the fix I was in. Toward going-home time I watched my chance, and when Vern was in a far corner with his back to the door, I slipped out, ran downstairs, found my things, and was just putting on the first rubber when I heard Vern's voice at the head of the stairs calling me.

I abandoned the second rubber, flew out of the schoolhouse, and ran all the way home (about a quarter of a mile), with one Sunday shoe getting all muddy, and with Vern running after me. But he was rather fat and didn't catch up with me until I reached our front porch. I suddenly remembered that I had heard Amy and May say that when a gentleman took you home, the proper thing was to invite him in, and since I certainly believed in being proper when it was feasible, I turned to Vern and said politely: "Won't you come in awhile?" He did, and stayed about a minute, then said he guessed he'd better be going.

When I told May the whole story, she laughed, then said it wouldn't have counted against me if, under such complicated circumstances, Vern had walked home with me. I was very disgusted with myself for not checking up on this in advance, for I never did get my other rubber, and the poor shoe that got so muddy never looked quite as shiny as the other one.

In the long run, however, that may have been constructive, for as long as that shoe lasted, it was a constant reminder that a person's brain is primarily meant for thinking.

CHAPTER III

Carrie Nation—More Drama—
The Hammock Scene

OUR NEXT MOVE was to Topeka, and I suppose this was done because it would be so much handier for most of us. Certainly for Dad, and for Rob and Walt, who worked there, and for May who had a new school out near Washburn College and could come home every night on her bicycle.

With May at home so much there seemed to be hardly anything left to wish for except that my hair would be naturally curly. But I didn't believe in wasting a wish on something with no hope at all attached to it.

Rex was ready for high school now, and Juanita and I were more than ready, but Juanita decided she had had enough education and got a job in a millinery shop. She was very popular with the boys, and probably figured she'd be getting married and what good would Latin and algebra do a wife and mother? Difficult enough to make a child obey if you stuck to plain English, and as for keeping a budget, all you needed to know was how to add and, particularly, subtract. (That sounds a bit facetious, but she did become a successful, contented wife and mother, with time to spare for various other activities.)

Mary and Elizabeth would of course go to the grade school in Topeka. Donald was too young for school, but at the age of three he was already a valuable member of our troupe of actors. And no anemic "Baa, baa, black sheep" for him, either; he could recite "Friends, Romans, countrymen," without a single mistake and, being a good mimic, with great eloquence, too, although of course he didn't understand a word of what he was saying.

Would Topeka be better or worse for Mother? Neither: she would fit in comfortably anywhere, even on the moon.

To make it perfect, the Overmyers moved to Topeka, too, just a few blocks from us.

Our house was big, fortunately, with thirteen people living in it (including Grandpa and Grandma), and soon a new stream of guests flowed in one door and out the other, not to mention our pals from Bellevue who came to see us. I don't remember much about little Donald's friends; the rest of us, from Elizabeth, with a few small girls mostly playing house, and Mary and Rex with a gang of boys and girls playing "Run, Sheep, Run" up to May with her beaux, kept things lively.

May had problems with her suitors and was usually unable to decide how much she liked them. She once spent the summer with our Aunt Alice in Colorado, chiefly to find out if she cared enough for her fiancé to go through with it; it turned out she didn't.

We also had a paying guest whom we called "the roomer." His name was Aron Hadley, and it would be impossible to say which fascinated me more, the name Aron or his pointed, light yellow, highly polished Sunday shoes. I never said anything more than "Hello" to him except once.

It was a soft summer evening and I sat on the porch steps, alone, pretending to myself that I couldn't bear to go in and leave the moon and stars, but actually hoping that Aron would come home and, finding me in that romantic setting, wouldn't be able to resist sitting down beside me.

He was a long time coming and I fell asleep. Suddenly I heard his step and jerking my head up, I exclaimed belligerently: "I wasn't asleep!"

He answered (and if I had written the line myself for one of our plays, I couldn't have done better): "Of course you weren't. It's too nice a night to neglect in sleep."

He neglected it, though, going right on into the house, which perhaps was just as well, as I am perfectly satisfied with my husband and way of life; no telling what I might have got into if I had married Aron. I do think, however, that he must have been a sensitive young man; there were any number of things he might have said which would have embarrassed a girl of fifteen.

The Dales had a room with us, too, for a while. Mr. Dale had just taken a job as traveling salesman and wasn't getting much of anywhere with it; someone told Mother of the hard time they were having. She gave Mrs. Dale and her little girl a room, and bought a small oil stove for them to cook on.

I can't remember how long they stayed with us, a matter of months, I imagine, but the interesting thing about it is that recently Rex got a letter from a woman in California, saying she read his books and had often wondered if he was the Rex Stout who had lived in Topeka, Kansas. If so, then his mother and father were the people who had taken her and her mother in when they were sadly up against it, and Rex and his brothers and sisters had opened up a new life for her.

She went on to say that she had been amazed to discover that some people actually considered the days as something to be enjoyed; she remembered that Elizabeth and Mary would set the alarm each night so that they could get up early and get their allotted tasks done, thus having more time to play, and that they had always included her in their fun. The shows in which we always gave her a part were like visits to Fairyland to her, she said, and she concluded with the remark that these experiences had changed her whole life.

Although this letter was gratifying, it was also somewhat disturbing, making it so plain that we are constantly influencing people in one way or another without wanting to or even knowing it. There is no way to avoid this unless we are willing to become hermits and it is foolish to think of it as a responsibility. Yet it is difficult to ignore.

Grandpa and Grandma Stout went to Chicago to live with Aunt Mary, Dad's sister. We missed Grandma's wonderful bread and pies, and Grandpa's wonderful personality.

A year or so later, Grandpa and Grandma Todhunter came to visit us. They lived in Ohio. I don't remember how long they stayed but it wasn't long enough for Grandpa to learn all of our names; most of the time it was "Sissy" to us girls and "Sonny" to the boys. We decided this was only mental laziness on his part since there were a number of reasons to believe he wasn't stupid.

I would like to tell how Grandpa Todhunter once handled a situation, when he had a guest who wouldn't accept a member of his household. For many years, until his death, a colored man lived with Mother's family and helped on the farm; Mother and her sisters and brothers called him Uncle Jack and, of course, he had his seat at the table in this family of good Quakers.

An old friend from the South came to Grandpa's for a visit, and when, going in to dinner the first day, he saw Uncle Jack about to take his accustomed place, the man was embarrassed and said in an aside to Grandpa: "I'm sorry, Amos, but I can't sit down to eat with that . . . that . . ."

Being a truly broadminded man, Grandpa realized that his friend was in a predicament; very likely he couldn't sit down to eat with a Negro without having indigestion or something worse. Not with criticism but with true understanding, Grandpa answered: "No, I guess thee can't. Let's see, which would thee rather do—have thy dinner in the kitchen now, or eat in here when we are finished?"

The trouble with telling that story is that I don't remember what the guest chose to do.

When I was sixteen I got the red kid gloves. They hadn't been difficult to earn; boys hadn't fallen over each other in an effort to win my favors. Perhaps one reason was that I relied too heavily on my beautiful soul; it's a bare possibility that I didn't have one to rely on.

When Mary got a little older, sometimes she and I would go to a party together, each with an escort. On a pleasant eve-

ning the customary procedure, when we returned home, was
for all of us to sit on the porch and talk awhile. This idea
didn't appeal to Mary much, and one night, after we sat for
about three minutes, she rose, muttering: "I'll take our hats
inside, Ruth."

She picked up the hats and went into the house and to bed,
and of course never heard the end of "taking in the hats."

There was a period (much too long a one) when Rex often
brought his best friend, Joe Lodge, and two other boys home
with him to stay all night. He had his own room with a large
bed and also a Morris chair in it, and three of the boys shared
the bed while the fourth slept in the chair. There was nothing
against this arrangement except that the bed broke down nearly
every time and fell with such a bang that it woke the household.
It was pretty awful to be wakened so often with a noise like a
thunderbolt. Of course the boys tried their best to fix the slats
so that they would support their weight, but they never did
succeed.

I think I was fifteen when Carrie Nation first came to our
house to dinner. May, Juanita and I joined her little army.
Mother was against drinking but she was also against violence,
so she didn't go on the smashing raids. She went to the meetings,
though, and Mrs. Nation often came to visit us.

It may surprise you to learn that she was a motherly little
woman, lovable, and with quite a sense of humor. That is,
I remember her as little—short and rather stocky—but I have
a way of thinking of people I like as small.

Anyway, I believe that many people have the mistaken notion that Carrie Nation was simply against drinking liquor, so
went about smashing saloons. But her whole point, at least in
Kansas, was that selling alcohol in that state was illegal, and
if the only way to make the citizens wake up to the fact that
the law was being broken was to smash the joints (the stores
which sold the liquor) —well, she would do some smashing and

cheerfully get locked up for her convictions. And she did do it cheerfully; I wish you could have seen her and the policemen laughing together, as they arrested her.

A smashing raid at daybreak was a great experience for a fifteen-year-old girl, eager to go to jail for a cause, but I had better save a description of that for my memoirs. I still have a scar on my right forefinger where broken fragments from the plate-glass window I smashed made the blood flow for right and justice; the disgusting part of it was that the policemen stood and watched me wielding my hatchet, then arrested only Mrs. Nation. Nothing for me to do but go home, get my finger bandaged, and dress for Sunday School.

The family began to grow smaller. May went to Chicago to study medicine. Rob went to New York. Walt went to Colorado for a while.

At last I was old enough to have a steady beau but my attitude toward boys was a little off the beaten path; for instance, it didn't occur to me that a boy liked me particularly just because he took me to parties and socials.

I did feel a little serious about one young man. He always took me home from Christian Endeavor, and one lovely summer evening, as we sat in the hammock on the porch, he leaned over and pulled me toward him. Even to me it was obvious what he had in mind, and I pushed him back—but tentatively —because I simply couldn't decide: was this the Prince or wasn't it?

He abandoned the project at once, but you would never guess what happened next. He said: "Ruth, I think you and I are both too emotional. Shall we pray for strength to resist temptation?"

So we bowed our heads in prayer, but, actually, he took care of it for both of us. Try my best, I wasn't able to enter in. Wrongly or rightly, I felt competent to handle my yieldings to that much temptation without having to bother God with it.

That was the end of my doubts about whether or not he was

my Prince. For one thing, could anyone with a sense of humor *do* that? For another, even if I loved him madly, who wanted to be married to a man who ran to God with every little detail? If we had the smallest disagreement, he would probably pray about it, and how would I make out, with two against me?

Our plays kept growing more and more popular. I don't remember how much we charged now, but I know it was no longer penny ante, and we gave several performances of each play in order to accommodate our audiences, even though we could seat fifty people at a time.

Two of our guests were indispensable at every performance: my brother Walt and a very good friend of mine, Mabel Foucht. Walt had to be there because his booming laugh was a guarantee that no witty dialogue would go unappreciated, and Mabel had to be sitting in the front row because at a play she cried at the slightest excuse and that set the right tone for the sad bits.

We were canny enough not to let either Mabel or Walt know why we generously gave them passes to every performance, for that might have made them self-conscious. Walt, as a matter of fact, was a good actor, but he wouldn't learn lines, wouldn't rehearse, and insisted on ad-libbing, so we had to get along without him.

Grace Overmyer came rushing into our house one day to report what she had overheard her mother telling a friend about our play of the previous night. Mrs. Overmyer had said: "Those children are really quite remarkable; they are superior to many of the professionals we see here. And the plays they write are surprisingly good."

For the next few days I went around in a dreamy haze and almost went into a decline, for when I'm unusually happy, I can't eat or sleep much.

We loved giving surprise parties, but I was the despair of everyone because I always guessed ahead of time when one was being planned for me. In fact I sometimes, optimist that I was, figured there was going to be a party when there wasn't. How-

ever, the night before I left Topeka, headed toward New York
in a search for Fame and the elusive Prince, I was given a surprise going-away party, and a number of the guests had arrived
before I realized what was going on.

On the train I began to feel a little scared and already a
little homesick, but I had learned in physics that two things
can't occupy the same place at the same time, so I deliberately
filled the small space in my head with romantic dreams.

I don't remember what they were, and I doubt if any of
them came true specifically. But why should dreams be expected
to come true? If they keep us happy while we're dreaming, isn't
that enough?

CHAPTER IV

A Distinguished Guest for Tea—
Dinner Served in Courses

I DIDN'T GET TO NEW YORK for five years. Rob and Tad (the pretty, lively telegraph operator he had married in New York) met me in Indianapolis, and for a week or two we had a wonderful time seeing shows and the like, then discovered that all of us were broke. I got a job with the telephone company, and when Rob and Tad moved on, I decided to let them go without me; their adventurous life—making their way from town to town, spending their last nickel on a play or an expensive dinner, pawning Tad's beautiful diamond ring—fascinated me but was too haphazard for a young girl who was out to *amount to something.*

I wondered where on earth Rob would land, with such a casual approach to life. Well, for those who may be interested, when he *did* land, he became a successful businessman, president of the New York Rotary Club, an official in a bank, and he now spends his winters in Florida. All of this may sound dull and unimaginative after such a carefree beginning, but I think he likes his life well enough, and besides, it hasn't made *him* dull at all.

Harriett Patrick, whom I nicknamed Pat, was one of the supervisors at the telephone company, and she and I became close friends. After awhile we took a room together. She was only seventeen (three years younger than I), but with her dignity and reticence looked and seemed much older; she had boosted her age to nineteen when she applied for the job.

Dad had left school work and was selling some product or other on the road; this wasn't his talent and it was heavy going

for him. He didn't get home very often. Elizabeth went to
Washington, D. C., to study nursing at a hospital there; Rex
went into the Navy as a yeoman and soon finagled himself onto
the *Mayflower*, President Theodore Roosevelt's yacht; May
was practicing medicine in Topeka; Walt had married a Topeka
girl, Gertrude Cathers, a very young, attractive brunette, and
he was now an efficient salesman for a large Chicago baking-
powder company; Juanita had a good job in a dry goods store;
Mary worked in a newspaper office.

Then Mother, Donald, and Mary decided to come to Indianapolis, with New York in mind, eventually, I think—at least
in Mary's. We rented a house and bought furniture on the installment plan. Pat lived with us.

It's odd but I can think of very few guests to tell about
through those years in Indianapolis. We were friendly with the
girls we worked with and some of them visited us but I don't
seem to remember a single party of any size; I don't think we
missed them, either, which is also odd.

We did have one distinguished guest. When Rex was in
New York, he wrote us that he and Julia Sanderson had become
good friends. In case you don't remember her, she was then
about the most popular musical-comedy star on Broadway. When
her show came to the English Opera House in Indianapolis
for two weeks, we sent her a note, inviting her to tea. We
were sure we were just wasting a stamp, so when her acceptance
arrived, we felt we were reading a novel which was going along
too smoothly to be true to life.

We three girls were quite worked-up at the prospect of entertaining a real actress, and a star to boot, but we couldn't,
to save ourselves, get Mother excited about it. The great day
came and so did the great lady. Everything went off perfectly
except that she bored us a little because she talked of nothing
but Rex. We knew all about him already; we wanted to hear
about her, and the theater, and New York.

We liked her, though; she even fascinated us to some extent,
but shortly after she had gone, Mary said wistfully: "We've

just entertained about the best that Broadway has to offer, yet I don't feel a bit different from the way I did this time yesterday, do you?"

Pat and I had to admit that we, too, were suffering from a flat feeling and even the prestige we achieved among our friends lasted only a short time.

One day I came across a surprising piece of information in a magazine for women: the proper way to serve a dinner was "in courses"; you didn't put everything on the table at once by any means. You started with some tasty thing called *hors d'oeuvres,* no other food on the table as yet; then you removed all traces of this course and served soup, then disposed of the soup plates. Next some fish, if it was a really stylish affair, and after more clearing away the meat and vegetables were served. Again more disposing of dishes, then the salad course. Finally you had dessert and coffee, but the coffee must be in special little cups and taken black. (Dad, who loved coffee and whose cup must be big and full, with lots of cream, would never have stood for that.)

I was quite impressed with all this and read it aloud to the folks. There was silence for a moment, then Mary asked: "Just when do you wash all those dishes? As you go along, or when it's all over?"

"When it's over, I guess, if you have enough to see you through," I replied, doubtfully.

"Shall we try it sometime?" Pat asked Mother.

"Of course, if you want to bother, but it does seem like a good deal to expect of one stomach," said Mother.

We did try it, one Sunday, when we were all at home to lend a hand, and I suppose you could call it a success although Mother was right, at least as far as I was concerned. Overeating always has given me a stomach ache. But I didn't get very sick, and we decided to try it on a guest the following Sunday.

We chose Blanche Stehlin, but didn't say a word to her about what was going to happen; it would have spoiled the effect if we had told her in advance. We decided to act as if that was our customary procedure, and as a matter-of-fact we had come to the conclusion that since that was the proper way to serve a meal, we had better do it always from now on; what if someone should drop in unexpectedly at mealtime and catch us eating like barbarians?

Dinner began, and Blanche tried to act as if she didn't notice anything peculiar, and managed splendidly up to the meat course; then amazement got the upper hand, and she demanded: "Mary, did you think this up?"

Pat and I merely raised our brows, as any lady would at a gauche remark from a guest, and Mary, the trooper, asked in a puzzled tone: "Think what up, Blanche?"

Then we took pity on her, and explained that this was the way "one" served dinner; we tactfully added that it was rather new and it wasn't surprising that she had never heard about it.

Not long after that, Blanche had us to dinner, and although that was some forty-odd years ago, I remember what her mother served: the best chicken and dumplings I have ever eaten, spinach, home-made grape jelly, lettuce salad, cherry pie, and coffee. A delicious meal but, to my amazement, no *hors-d'oeuvres*, no soup or fish, and the salad served with the chicken. How astonishing, I thought, that after we had shown Blanche the proper way to serve a dinner, she hadn't told her mother.

I suppose few of us escape being somewhat snobbish in our youth, but I recall now with distaste that supercilious girl who sat at a friend's table and felt superior while eating with relish.

Our stylish meals were destined to be short-lived; Donald, ten years old, dealt them their death blow. He was deep in a book one evening when we called him to dinner and he said: "Tell me when you get as far as the meat; I can't fool around with all that other stuff."

That was enough. Later, we asked Mother why she hadn't pointed out to us at the start that it was silly to waste all that time and effort and she replied: "The best way to learn is to catch your own mistakes."

CHAPTER V

Guests Seem to Multiply

ONE DAY WE GOT A TELEGRAM saying May had died in her sleep. I have never loved anyone else quite the way I cared for her, and that's all I want to say about that.

Pat had recently gone back to her hometown, Utica, N.Y., and was to be married shortly. Rex was out of the Navy now, and he and Rob and Tad were living in New York. They wrote and urged Mother, Mary, Donald and me to go there, so we did, a month before Christmas, 1909. Dad said he would come for the holidays, and try to find work in New York.

The boys had a furnished apartment on Morningside Avenue ready for us; Mother would have some trees nearby, in the park across the street. This was important, although I don't think it would be fair to her to say she could hardly have managed without them; I'm sure she could have, very nicely. But it's difficult to imagine her without some green, growing thing near at hand.

We became friendly with several of the other families in the apartment house and went to dances and parties with some of the young people. We also made friends with some of our co-workers; I was in the office of Franklin Simon & Co. and grew very fond of the head bookkeeper, Flora Currick, an attractive Jewish girl.

One Saturday Flora went home to lunch with me, and that afternoon we and the two girls who lived in the flat above us went over to the park to hear the band concert. After one of the pieces, Flora remarked: "I love that Oriental music."

Not realizing that Flora *looked* Jewish or that the piece the band had just played had any relation to Hebrew music, I had no idea what was in their minds when I noticed the two girls with us glance at each other with a smug, knowing kind of smile.

But Flora understood and explained to me later. I couldn't believe what she told me and set out to prove she was wrong by one day casually questioning one of the girls. Flora was right, and I was speechless with wonder; I had lived for twenty-seven years without realizing there was actually such a thing as religious prejudice.

It is high time to bring in some famous guest, if only I can scare one up. Well, you younger people may never have heard of Eugene Manlove Rhodes; he was writing stories of the West at this time for *The Saturday Evening Post*. He had been a cowboy, and still was, I believe. He had had little formal education, but his stories were superior, and so was he.

Rob had him to dinner one evening at his apartment, next door to us, and brought him over to meet us afterward. In the conversation, one of us said something like: "By that time she will have done so many things . . ." and Mr. Rhodes remarked in all seriousness: "I'd give a hundred dollars if I could come through with that 'will have done' as offhand as that."

Wouldn't anybody like a successful writer who was as unpretentious as that?

After a few years we moved to a four-story brownstone house on West 118th Street, about half a block from Morningside Park. We all had fairly good jobs now (except Donald, who was in school), but even so, I don't know where we got the fancy idea of taking such a place, or where we found the money and the courage to try to furnish it.

I remember that the only thing we bought on the installment plan was a player-piano. Once, when ready cash was no doubt scarce, Rex received a bill from the piano dealer with a note attached which read: "Dear Mr. Stout: Will you please send us your check for this amount, or one of your witty notes, telling why you can't? We don't much care which."

The basement floor of our house was the kitchen and dining room and the two top ones were bedrooms. The floor you entered from the high front stoop had just two rooms, one rather good-sized and the other immense. We called the smaller one the library; there was a table, some chairs, a large couch, some bookcases and a fireplace in there. But in the larger room there was only the player-piano; we called it the "ballroom," and used it only for dancing when we had parties.

We really needed a large house. Juanita had married Walter Roddy in Topeka and a year later they had come East with Walter, Jr. and were living on Long Island; they now had a little Juanita, too, and when they all came to stay overnight, we could put them up comfortably. Elizabeth was home again, now, a graduate nurse, and Walt and Gertrude and their cute daughter, Ruth Merle, came to see us a few times a year.

Uncle Oscar arrived from Ohio for an indefinite stay and our cousin, Adda, came from Colorado for some specialized studying and of course stayed with us. She introduced us to Ed Carlson, also from Denver, who was taking singing lessons, with opera in mind. He became so much one of the family that although he continued to pay rent somewhere else, oftener than not be shared Rex's bedroom.

To these intermittent regulars we have to add those who came to a party or to dinner on a cold, wintry night and didn't want to go home. Or even on a warm moonlit night.

I remember that after one party we girls were tired and wanted to go to bed but the boys wanted a few more dances, and our wide stairway became a battleground, the girls clinging to the bannisters, determined to get upstairs, the boys hanging on to their ankles and skirts, trying to pull them back to the "ballroom."

One Sunday morning, after a late party, Walt and Don were still in bed at breakfasttime on the double couch in the library, and the family and a few overnight guests were all gathered there, trying to persuade them to get up, because breakfast wouldn't be half as much fun without them. Those two when they collaborated could make anyone shout with laughter (even themselves) and they now completely ignored us and lay there making up silly rhymes, such as:

> The very best guns are made by Krupp
> But that don't mean we're gonna get up.

Lovey, our colored maid, after having called a few threats from the basement, finally climbed the stairs to issue an ultimatum: come to breakfast right now or go hungry. Walt and Don began making up verses about her and she stood there shaking with laughter until the tears streamed down her face.

Once in awhile, old friends from Kansas would show up. When Julia Parker (not her real name) wrote that she was coming to New York with a cousin whom we had never met, we recalled how Julia had always enjoyed jokes, even when they were on her, so we decided to think up something to amuse her.

We would give a *la-de-da* dinner party. Uncle Oscar looked almost exactly like Chauncey Depew, so he would be Chauncey, and Ed Carlson looked a great deal like Ricardo Martin, a tenor singing at the Metropolitan that season. With his rich tenor voice, Ed could play the role of Martin flawlessly.

Every man we knew begged to be the butler; we chose a tall, dignified friend of Rob's—a banker, if you please. Naturally we girls would doll up in evening dresses, and Elizabeth took one of hers to Mother and asked her if she would wear it. "Tut, tut, child," replied Mother.

Julia and her cousin arrived early in the afternoon. The latter was a stodgy, diffident woman, without a word to say; we had never seen her before so just accepted that, but Julia! How changed she seemed! New York, or something, apparently overwhelmed her; she acted ill at ease, out of place, almost scared.

We telephoned Ed and the butler, telling them not to dare show up even in their normal characters; Uncle Oscar was allowed to come to the table, but just as himself he seemed a little frightening to the two women.

Lovey was given a vacation for a few days; the seeming terror of our guests was catching and we were afraid they wouldn't be able to survive our having a maid. Of course there was nothing we could do about living in a four-story house, but we did hasten to say that the reason we didn't have any furniture in the large front room was because we couldn't afford to buy any, which, come to think of it, must have been close to the truth.

That experience with Julia bothered us for a while. Naturally, we knew that her actions weren't necessarily caused by the contrast between the Middle West and New York City; our cousin Adda, Ed Carlson, and other people we knew had come straight out of the West and hadn't been intimidated by New York. We had fitted in with Julia once and now we didn't. Why was this?

We found no definite answer, but were convinced that under no circumstances, in no environment, would we and she ever again find a common meeting ground.

I think we were mistaken. I believe we could give something to, and get something from, the majority of human beings if only we knew how to do it, and I've thought up a few simple rules which help me.

One is: don't look for what isn't there. It has been said that you can't get blood from a turnip and that's true enough, but why should you expect to? If blood is what you're looking for, buy a piece of liver.

I don't expect the person who thinks Hemingway ranks with Dostoevsky to share my taste in literature, but that needn't mean that we have no other taste in common. And the girl who never had to earn her living can't be expected to feel anything more than a vague and superficial sympathy for you if you have just lost your job, but maybe you both love cats.

It is quite true that I wouldn't care to spend a lot of time with the woman whose main point of contact with me was a discussion of recipes, and I would also shy away from several straight evenings with almost any member of the intelligentsia; the chances are he would bore me. Neither do I think I would be interesting company to many people for a number of successive evenings. In other words, take a little from this one, a little from that one, but don't be greedy.

Another rule I follow religiously is: don't force yourself to spend time with people you don't enjoy. If you hate spinach, don't eat it; try beet tops. On the other hand, the more people you can give to, and take from, the richer you are. The exclusive people, surely, are the ones who live the narrow lives.

And now back to Julia Parker for a moment. We once enjoyed her and I believe that if she was now living across the road from us, secure in her own environment, we might find there was still some definite point of contact between us.

I don't remember why we moved from 118th Street but after a few years there, we took a large apartment at 101st Street and Central Park West. Mother could again see trees and grass from our front windows; perhaps that was why we moved.

Pat, whose husband had died, came from Utica and lived with us for a year or two, and Isabel Turner, a nurse, shared Elizabeth's room for a number of years.

One summer, Ethel Chapman, my childhood pal, came to New York from Topeka to take a course at Columbia; she and another teacher had rented a furnished apartment near the college and Ethel's mother and her cousin, Fay Kennedy, came for a visit. One Sunday I asked them all to breakfast, and also invited A. J. Stout (no kin to us) of Topeka; he was spending the summer in New York. He had been my teacher in physics and I and many other high school youngsters had worked diligently in an effort to earn a word, or even a smile, of praise from him. In those days I would never have believed that he and I would both, one day, be in New York and I would invite him to my home. Even then I felt a little fluttery about it.

At that time Rex was writing short stories and had rented

a small room downtown where he could work without interruption; I wouldn't have asked him to come all the way uptown to breakfast if I hadn't wanted to serve muskmelons. He was much better at choosing them than any of the rest of us, and if you have lived in Kansas where the standard is high (and particularly if you have grown your own there), you are fussy about the melon you serve, especially to Kansans. So I asked Rex if he would mind coming and bringing some melons.

During the meal he made some youthfully cynical remark about falling in love—by gosh, he would never be caught doing anything as inane as that—at which Mr. Stout smiled and said: "I wish I could be there when it happens."

Well, he *was,* for at that very moment Rex was falling hard for Fay, and it's possible that his remarks were prompted by a vague feeling of impending defeat; perhaps he was putting up a fight against a sensation of eventual subjugation.

When, shortly after breakfast, Fay said she had to leave, and asked how to get to the subway. Rex offered to go with her and put her on the right train. Elizabeth and Mary and I exchanged glances, for although Rex did many things for his sisters which were the envy of those of our friends who had less unselfish brothers, he had long ago made it clear that he wouldn't take our various girl friends home, or even to a streetcar.

The upshot of that short walk to the subway was that Fay didn't leave for home the next day, as she had planned to do, and she and Rex became engaged with lightning speed.

Mr. Stout was amused when I told him, but I was sobered; Rex and Fay would be married because I hadn't trusted myself to select some melons. How did people dare to live when such a small thing could result in such big consequences?

Mother and Dad had both gone to college but their children had not been willing to waste time sitting around in a college classroom when Life was right there on the doorstep challenging us to come on out and see what we could do with it. And yet we all took it for granted that Donald would go to college, so it was upsetting to discover that he often played hookey from his high school classes.

We talked it over, then because Donald (twelve years younger than I) had always been my charge, I asked to be the one to speak to him. I told him that Mother and Dad weren't the kind of parents you concealed things from; you simply told them what you wanted to do, and unless you were planning to rob a bank or commit a murder, the chances were that they would tell you to go ahead and follow your Inner Light.

It turned out that he had been spending his time running errands (without pay) for the keepers at the Bronx Zoo. Because of his love for all animals and the great number of animal books he read, we might have guessed that he was up to something like that. He was allowed to quit school and spent all his time at the Zoo. He was planning to be a big game hunter some day; that is, to capture animals and bring them back alive.

One day he asked Mother if he could invite a very special person to dinner the following evening; this man was a member of the staff of the Museum of Natural History, and was leaving in a few days on an expedition. Mother agreed and Donald was in a state of bliss.

As it turned out, the only ones at home that evening were Mother and Donald; the guest arrived and kept both of them enthralled during the meal with his tales of adventure.

Perhaps at this point I should explain that, not counting her talent for creating a minor banquet out of a few leftovers, Mother was not a particularly good cook; she would occasionally take an interest in some diet or other, with an emphasis on simplicity and health, but aside from that, there were any number of things in the world which she found more provocative than food.

This night, after the illustrious guest had departed, Donald said something to Mother (jokingly, so as not to hurt her feelings) about the unusualness of having only potatoes and dessert for dinner for a guest.

It always took a rather drastic thing to upset Mother, but that did it. With a gasp, she took Donald to the kitchen, opened the oven door and showed him the luscious roast she had forgotten to serve, the peas in a pot on the stove, the salad in the ice-box.

"We will have him again, Donald," she said, "and will warn him not to begin his adventure stories until all the food is safely on the table."

Donald never got to Africa. He died a few years later of tuberculosis, with the nurses, doctors, and other patients at the sanitarium who had grown fond of him, so distressed that Mother tried to comfort them; she assured them that he was all right, and that those who had loved him hadn't lost him.

"His humor, his enthusiasm, his zest for living—gone," muttered one doctor, but Mother replied: "No. As long as we remember these things, they are not gone."

"He wanted to live," sobbed a nurse in furious protest, and Mother replied: "He *is* living."

CHAPTER VI

Greenwich Village—A Hypnotist—Russia

KITTY MORTON, a lifelong friend of Mother's youngest sister, was a red-haired, attractively homely woman who liked to run about over the earth to see what everyone was doing. She had a small income and was constantly going broke because of some trip she couldn't resist. When I first met her she was about fifty years old. She had just returned from Egypt, and came to our house to dinner one night—a guest who changed my whole life.

She told us fascinating things about various places she had seen, then got started on Greenwich Village, a section of New York which had oddly enough escaped our attention. The following afternoon she and I went to the Mad Hatter for tea. At that time the Village was almost a private little world of its own, with few restaurants and only one or two tea rooms. It was rarely invaded by "foreigners" (uptowners) and many a Villager prided himself on never having ventured above 14th Street.

At this point my time was my own; I was making a living, of sorts, writing short stories. Aside from the modest amount we each paid in at home, I had so far made just enough money to buy a new typewriter. But *what* a typewriter! Never short on imagination, I had had the vulgar keys (the dollar mark, percent sign, etc.) changed to French accent marks and the German umlaut, in spite of the fact that my French was scanty and at that time I hadn't even a desire to learn German. Too, I had little patience with fictional characters who had a passion for showing off the author's knowledge of a foreign language.

However, my characters had a disconcerting habit of coming out with unexpected remarks; what if one of them should suddenly say: *"Elle est très triste"* and there was no accent mark on the typewriter to complete the *très*. What a fix I would be in!

I went overboard for Greenwich Village and when Kitty asked me if I would open a tearoom with her, I said "Certainly," although the nearest thing I had to capital was a story which had been rejected four times. Nothing to pawn, at last I understood why foresighted women bought diamonds when they had some idle money.

Kitty also had very little money just then, and what a gay old time we had, searching for usable junk in second-hand stores for our Will-O-The-Wisp, the tearoom we had together for about a year! We separated, then, because we weren't making enough to support two people. Kitty kept the Wisp, and I opened the Klicket and ran it for a year or two.

The people who came into these two tearooms could be called guests (not always paying ones, unfortunately), so the Greenwich Village adventures technically belong here, but since they would make a whole book by themselves, I will have to leave them out. However, a few of the people became my friends, and one became my husband, so I will tell you briefly about them.

Husband first: Fred Rossiter's wife came into the Wisp one afternoon for tea and liked it so much that she brought Fred in that same evening. My Prince for sure! We fell in love at once but didn't get married until thirteen years later.

Unfortunately I can't do Fred justice here; it is permissible to rave on about how marvelous other people are, but poor taste, I believe, to laud one's husband or wife, so I'll just say that he still suits me fine and let it go at that.

I had made some good friends during the past eight years, but no close one except Rex's wife, Fay; now there were others: Jocelyn Tabois (Tabby), Elizabeth Bankson (Binkie), Kay Powell, a Topeka girl, Susan Townsend, and Joe Coffey. All except Joe were artists.

Tabby was a fascinating Englishwoman, who looked like Ellen Terry; she suspected (and was right) that she had little talent for painting. Her sense of humor was boundless. She and her son, Leo, had an apartment in Patchin Place. While I had the Klicket, Tabby spent most of her waking hours there; when I gave it up, I could usually be found at her place, when not at work. I did go home to sleep.

This was during the first World War; I have never known anyone to hate war with the passion that Tabby did.

She and her son returned to England about thirty-five years ago, and I visited them there, both in London and Cornwall, once. It has now been a long time since I have heard from Tabby; I feel sure she can't have survived the fury and scorn which must have possessed her at the progress war has made. The expert bombing of defenseless people, and all the rest of it.

If she is alive, she without a doubt makes many a caustic observation about the patriots who unprotestingly let their sons leave for war, to kill and be killed for their country, while they themselves go to great lengths to avoid paying income tax. I can still hear the scorn in her throaty voice when she told of how her husband wanted their seventeen-year-old son to enlist, yet was indignant when she suggested they donate their phonograph to the soldiers.

There was Elizabeth Bankson (Binkie) who had come to New York from Erie, Pa., to study art. She found her way into the Wisp one night, a short slender girl, with gorgeous dark-red hair and intelligent brown eyes. I liked her soft voice, but I soon realized she would have got further with a louder one. Many Villagers didn't go into a tearoom for tea, and often didn't pretend to order any; they came in to tell anyone who would listen what was what in the realm of ideas, and although Binkie's head was full of interesting, original contributions, her small voice too often went unheard in the din of more assertive, louder ones.

Susan Townsend was an attractive Southern girl who made her living illustrating children's books. Her voice was as gentle as Binkie's.

Through Fay I met Kay Powell, a Topeka girl, tall, rangy,

likable. A successful artist, chiefly murals. (Both Kay and Susan are so averse to publicity that I'm not using their real names.)

And Joe Coffey, that tall, good-looking Irishman who could (and did) wear a suit turning green with age and yet look as though he had just stepped out of Saville Row. His life was complicated: he wasn't living with his wife, they had four children, there was a girl with whom he was in love, and he had no money. His father, a multi-millionaire, had left his affairs in a terrible tangle when he died; Joe, waiting for the estate to be straightened out, was always expecting to have plenty any day, which kept him from settling down to earning a living.

I wasn't the girl with whom Joe was in love, but some such rumor no doubt found its way up to our home on Central Park West, for Joe practically lived at the Klicket.

He did have some sort of a job in Jersey for a time, and he had a room near where he worked. One Saturday evening when he and I were at Tabby's, he said he hated to go back to Jersey that night, but confessed he had no money to pay for a hotel room. (This was after I had given up the Klicket, where he and a few others sometimes used the benches for a bed, when they had no better place to sleep.) I remembered that Mother had gone to Rob's home to stay a few days, and since she had a room to herself, I took Joe home with me and he slept in her bed.

The next morning Dad, as usual, got up early and prepared his own breakfast; a little later, when we girls were in the kitchen, he called me into his room.

"That fellow, Joe Coffey, is here, isn't he? Is he going to be here for dinner today?"

Dad had never met Joe and I was astonished at his belligerent tone.

"Why—why—I don't know," I stammered.

"Well, find out; if he is, I'll eat out somewhere."

I was dumfounded. Never had I heard Dad take such an attitude to any of his children since we had grown up. He wasn't a typical Quaker; on the contrary, he was peppery and excitable, so it was all the more to his credit that he so seldom interfered in our lives, letting us do what the spirit moved us to do.

I went back to the kitchen in a sort of daze and told the girls what he had said; they were as nonplussed as I was.

Joe was in his room, dressing. I knew how sensitive he was to the moods and attitudes of others, and if Dad should meet him in the hall and give him an unfriendly glare from his snappy black eyes, I was certain Joe would suddenly remember a pressing date and vanish. Having reached the street, he would probably toss up his last nickel to decide which: cup of coffee or subway downtown. With the kind of luck that followed him around, I was also sure the nickel would roll through a grating on the street.

There was no alternative, I had to appease Dad. But how do you approach a father who has suddenly stepped out of character? I returned to his room, desperately, not hopefully.

"Listen, Dad," I told him.

"You listen to me," he ordered, then didn't know what to say next, unaccustomed as he was to telling us off.

I took advantage of his predicament. Banking on Joe's irresistible appeal (almost a tangible thing) for both men and women, I said quickly: "One of your best traits, Dad, is a sense of fairness, and whatever you have against Joe must be hearsay. Won't you meet him and judge him for yourself?"

He was silent for a moment, then said: "All right. I'll meet him."

A few minutes later I took Joe into the livingroom, where Dad was standing, gazing out at the park. I introduced them, then left, feeling sure they would do better without me.

We delayed operations a little. After about fifteen minutes Elizabeth went in and told Joe to come to breakfast. They started for the diningroom, but Dad called Elizabeth back.

"I asked Mr. Coffey to stay to dinner. I told him two o'clock," he said, trying to be casual. "What are we having for dessert?"

Delighted, Elizabeth murmured: "Well, I'm not sure . . . I think . . ."

"Better have some ice cream. I'll bring it when I come back from meeting." Then he muttered, half to himself: "Wonder what flavors he likes. Guess I better get several."

Late that afternoon, when Joe had gone, Dad said to me: "I have lived a long time and have met a great many men but I have never seen a finer gentleman than Mr. Coffey."

There was no mistaking his sincerity, and I wasn't in the least surprised, for that was what Joe did to everyone. If I undertook to explain this, it would take a chapter or two, and then I would probably fail, but this I know: it isn't that elusive and superficial thing called charm, although Joe has more than his share of that, too; his appeal is of the spirit.

As I have said, Dad's normal attitude to our goings-on, unorthodox as some of them were, was one of acceptance. There was another Sunday morning when he got up and found that there were two young men (strangers to him) asleep on the livingroom floor, with me, fully dressed, asleep on the couch.

This is how it happened: On Saturdays I often kept the Klicket open long past midnight, for that was the evening when many uptowners (who at that period had just begun to discover the Village) went "slumming," and this was my opportunity to take in enough cash to pay the rent and keep the place in candles. One moonlit Saturday night (or, rather, Sunday morning) Tacheechee (a full-blooded Indian, a good artist, and the first person I had met in the Village) and Dennis (a pleasant young man, who thought of himself as a poet, and may have been) decided it would be a pity to go home on such a fine night, so they rode uptown with me on the El. When we reached our place, it still seemed too nice to go inside, and we went across the street and into Central Park.

We stood by the lake, wishing we could take a boat ride, but the boats were tied up, out of reach. Tach announced that he was going to swim out and untie one, and he dived into the water in his clothes, came back in a boat and took us for a splendid row. Splendid, that is, for Dennis and me; poor Tach shivered through it all.

I couldn't let him go back downtown in wet clothes, so we went up to our apartment. I got a bathrobe and gave it to Tach; he stripped in the kitchen, put on the robe and draped his clothes over a chair or two, while Dennis spread his wet paper money out on the kitchen table.

There were no empty beds so the men stretched out on the rug in the livingroom and were soon asleep. That was no innovation; every now and then we had so many guests that one or more of us slept on the floor.

At that time Pat was sharing my room. She was a light sleeper, so, rather than disturb her at that hour, I lay down on the livingroom couch.

When Dad got up (always before anyone else), he put Tach's clothes on hangers and transferred the money to another table out of his way. When he woke us up with his clatter he asked us to have breakfast with him. Tach and Dennis were quite impressed; they assured me that most fathers would at least have raised an eyebrow.

Elizabeth was taking a course in psychology at Columbia and was full of enthusiasm for her teacher's ideals. We girls decided that a word of appreciation was in order and since I seemed to be constantly writing to some stranger about something or other, it took no coaxing to get me to write to this one, praising him for his excellent point of view.

I got in return a note which didn't quite escape being flowery. The idealist (never mind his name) was delighted to hear from someone who was also searching for the rare flower of something or other (I can't just remember what), and he wanted to know me. He asked me to choose some church where we could meet.

The church idea was, we thought, his delicate way of letting me know that his intentions were of the loftiest. The girls urged me to suggest The Little Church Around The Corner, since it was famous for the romances which had been completed there. But I didn't want to frighten him away before I had looked him over, so, having heard that Dr. Percy Stickney Grant was an interesting speaker, I chose his church.

I wrote, suggesting a date, evening service, and added I would be wearing a navy blue suit with a yellow rose in the jacket lapel. He replied that he would be there.

Elizabeth and Mary went too, of course, and took seats a few rows back of me. A short time after we arrived, a young man came and bent over me. "Are you Miss Stout?" he asked.

I nodded and he sat down beside me and remarked: "Do you know the subject of the sermon tonight?" I said no, and he handed me a leaflet with the subject printed at the top in large letters: "What Are We Here For?"

The girls could hardly wait until I got home to find out how I had made out, and what he had said at the very first to make me laugh. When I told them, Elizabeth said, in a worried tone: "But it didn't seem funny to him."

"No, it didn't," I admitted gloomily. "There were other indications that he's definitely shy on a sense of humor, but even so, I asked him to tea next Sunday."

Well, that little romance didn't jell. I'm sure he had a fine character, but no appeal for any of us, and it is much more than likely that we had none for him, either.

We invited one person to our home who never came. One of our friends, in an effort to get a better secretarial job, advertised in one of the papers; she showed us a letter she received in reply from some man who didn't need a secretary, he said, but would like very much to correspond with her. We decided it would be fun to find out what his angle was, and I was again appointed to do the writing.

I sent him a short note, and in reply received a polite, very interesting letter. We corresponded for a few weeks. Then another girl we knew, who had also advertised, happened one day to show me a letter *she* had received in reply to *her* advertisement from a man asking her to correspond with him. It was from the same one.

This was, naturally, an opportunity which I couldn't pass

up, so I now wrote to him under two names. I don't remember how long this went on; all of his letters were interesting, they weren't repetitious, and not by the slightest hint did he suggest he wanted to meet either girl.

Finally I sent him a gay note, inviting him to a small party, and I signed both names, thus letting him in on the secret. We could have wept at his reply, and I think we did: he declined our invitation, saying he was deaf and dumb.

Another stranger whom we invited to the house was a French hypnotist whose stage name was Pauline. In private life he was Dr. Joseph Poulin. He was incredibly attractive and a Broadway matinee idol for several seasons, beginning early in 1910.

The story of how Rob's wife, Tad, and Mary and I used fancy and strategic measures to get him to take some interest in us, and of how we succeeded when any number of other girls were turning themselves inside out just for an autographed picture of him is too long to tell here, and I'm sorry; it's quite a tale.

The Sunday papers at that time often carried full-page spreads about him, and now and then there was a scientific article by him on hypnotism. So many of his pictures were stolen from the theater lobby (and I'm not admitting who started that custom) that they were finally put under glass. It was reported that he received hundreds of letters every week which he couldn't find time to answer, so it wasn't surprising that we felt somewhat smug when he took the trouble to find out who we were. In our communications we signed fictitious names and gave no addresses.

This all started during our first winter in New York, when we knew almost no one; I suppose we substituted these antics for the social life which, under other circumstances, would have been taking up our leisure time. Having started, we kept it up until finally it reached the point where Pauline, at the height of his popularity, tried to meet us. A friend of his (whom we didn't know), Mr. Zittell of *Zit's Weekly,* a theatrical paper, made the advances, but we declined, saying the whole thing would probably lose its spice if we actually met Pauline; we preferred things as they were.

Our interest died a natural death, and Pauline's popularity finally petered out. Then, some years later, he reappeared, not on Broadway but at a Brooklyn theater, which was an indication of what had happened to his prestige. We went over to see him perform for old times' sake, and found he was still attractive. But the spark in us was so definitely dead that, with nothing to lose, we wrote him, asking him to Sunday supper, and he accepted.

We decided to make a party of it. Juana Lord, a friend from Topeka, was staying with us at that time, and we asked Rex and Fay, Binkie, and Joe Coffey, to come and assist at these last rites.

I didn't eat meat at that time and Juana made me promise to conceal that fact; she insisted that a person had to know me well to realize I didn't have the *soul* of a vegetarian.

To start things off about as unfortunately as possible, that Sunday was the first day of daylight-saving time. Pauline was asked for five o'clock; he arrived promptly and we had forgotten to change our clocks. I answered his ring, and my surprise at what I thought was his early arrival disconcerted him, and my attire (a robe) disconcerted me.

It was an extremely high tea with plenty of good food, and I don't suppose you could call it a failure since nobody was aiming at anything. Pauline mentioned his place in the country and then he and Rex were off—discussing cows, pigs, skunks, and things. I didn't have to pretend to eat meat, for Pauline paid scant attention to me.

That was the last we heard of him until years later, when we read that he and some friends, at a party in a hotel, were arrested for throwing a waiter out of a third-story window, while they sang "Out the window you must go." By good luck, the man landed on a canopy and wasn't badly hurt, but Pauline and his drinking companions were promptly carted off to the police station.

I was married to Fred when this happened, and don't imagine for a minute that he didn't make the most of it. I insisted that if there was any truth in the story at all, Pauline must have been just an innocent bystander.*

Back to the tearoom days. Fred's first marriage hadn't been a success, and he had thought he would have no difficulty getting a divorce. It didn't turn out that way, however, and we decided neither to see each other nor to write.

Naturally I wasn't in a very happy frame of mind about this, and to try to divert me Rex suggested that I go to hear Scott Nearing lecture. He was an economist, teacher, and lecturer, and I first heard him talk at the Rand School of Social Science on Current Events.

This book is getting a little cluttered up with fascinating men, so I will just say about Scott that, later, after I had become his secretary, I enjoyed teasing him by assuring him that it wasn't his interesting ideas that packed halls to standing room only whenever he talked; it was his voice, smile and personality.

After I had attended a few of his lectures I did a little conniving, and by the time I went to Russia for the Quakers in 1923 to do famine relief work, he and I were friendly, although more on a mutual "Save The World" basis than anything more personal.

We corresponded while I was gone and what a disappointment my letters must have been to him! Instead of endeavoring to give him a blow-by-blow account of what was cooking in the Kremlin (and that, of course, was why he was corresponding with me) I went on about how happy Ivan was with the cow I had managed to scrape up money for, and I told him that Masha's operation had been successful, and that I had collected

---

* Footnote by Fred: He was taken to jail, wasn't he?

enough money from friends at home to send Seryozha to a Conservatory of Music. It took poor Scott quite awhile to realize that, although I recognized the vital importance of his activities and interests, I just wasn't politically-minded and never would be.

Shortly after I returned from Russia, Elizabeth and I went to hear Scott; he saw us in the audience, and sent someone to ask me to wait for him after the lecture. I felt like the Queen of the May, although I well knew that all he wanted was to find out what he could about Russia; at that time only Quakers were allowed in the Soviet Union.

Scott asked if we had time to go somewhere for something to eat and a talk, but I suggested (with diffidence, for he was, after all, my hero) that he go home with us for supper, instead. He agreed so nonchalantly that I thought: Gosh, why didn't I ask him long ago?

Mother was the only one at home; I introduced her to Scott, then Elizabeth and I went to the kitchen to prepare as fine a supper as we could for our distinguished guest.

Scott was forty years old at that time, Mother was seventy. In a few minutes they were buddies. We sat down to the meal, and Scott and Mother continued their formidable discussion of international affairs or something of the sort. At one point, Scott made some statement or other, and Mother reached over and patted his arm with friendly tolerance. "Tut, tut, Sonny. You have quite a lot to learn," she said.

Elizabeth and I almost gasped, but Scott sort of opened up like a flower after that; it had no doubt been a long time since anyone outside of his family had treated him as an equal. There is something a little stark and forbidding about adoration, and trying to keep one's balance on a pedestal must be a very undesirable and difficult job.

Scott and Mother became such special friends that, years later, when she had a cottage built on our place in Connecticut, just an S O S from her would bring him all the way from his place in Vermont to help her with some difficulty. He was an expert builder and farmer and whether Mother's problem concerned a fireplace or a peach tree, Scott could help her and loved to.

Louis Fuchs, a colorful Hungarian (who had been a stowaway on a ship coming to America at the age of eleven, and had made his way here ever since) was one of my most satisfying friends during that difficult period after Fred and I parted. Louis was likable, amusing, and such an individualist that he was constantly doing crazy unexpected things which took my mind off my own affairs.

Just one incident about him, although there are dozens. The first time I asked him to dinner, I had three other guests, who had known Louis much longer than I had. He wasn't a social person in the conventional sense, that is, it was an achievement to get him to even accept this sort of invitation at all. When, that particular evening, the dinner hour came and went and he hadn't arrived, his friends assured me he wouldn't show up.

He did, however, finally, and we sat down to the meal, the first course of which was soup. Louis didn't even pretend to eat it.

"How do you know you don't like it, Louis? You haven't even tasted it," someone said.

With his soup-spoon he carefully lifted bits of meat and vegetables from the bowl in front of him and gazed at them suspiciously.

"I don't eat nothin' I can't call by name," he said, amiably.

I had tried to fix a very good dinner which included an expensive steak because I knew Louis was a fussy eater, but he scarcely touched it. I was exasperated.

"You can call the steak by name and I've heard you say you love it and this one is good. Why on earth don't you eat it?" I demanded.

He glanced at me with dark eyes which always looked a little sad even when they twinkled with humor as they now did.

"Listen, how did I know what you might try to make me eat—you a vegetarian? I had me a fine steak at Luchow's on my way up here." He gave the piece of cold steak on his plate a friendly poke with his fork, and added, generously: "It wasn't no better than this one, though."

CHAPTER VII

Poverty Hollow and Here They Come!

TEN YEARS PASSED, Fred got a divorce and we were married in June. In September we bought a fifty-five-acre place in Poverty Hollow, Redding Ridge, Conn. Six months later, on March 28th, 1930, we moved to our farm.

There was an immense barn on the place not far from the house which we converted into living quarters for our friends. Mother always called it "The Lodge." The lower floor was made into four bedrooms, kitchen, large livingroom, a shower, toilet, and a lavatory. The huge loft was left untouched, empty.

The bedrooms were small and Spartan, with two narrow beds, a chair, and dresser in each. We bought a dozen good woolen blankets to add to the few old ones we had. The kitchen contained shelves, an oil range, a small coal stove for heating water, a table, chair, old-fashioned icebox, some pots, pans, and dishes. The livingroom was furnished with odds and ends. This was at the beginning of the depression when money was scarce and I guess we figured that if the guests wanted extra comforts they would have to provide them.

For that matter, our own house was far from luxurious. Before we left New York we got rid of anything which would have been a burden and out-of-place in a home where simplicity was to be the keynote—a large, light-colored, expensive Chinese rug, for instance. We kept some attractive things but nothing which would take much looking after.

We had an invitation printed which said that the recipient was welcome to come to the barn whenever there was a vacant bed and stay as long as he liked, but he would have to furnish his own linen and food, and do his own work.

There were several reasons for the barn arrangement. For one thing, our house at that time could accommodate only four beds; there was room for only two guests. In winter that would be all right, but during the summer months what on earth would we do with our families and friends who were all eager for us to get settled so they could come to see us? Also, I was planning to have a large flower and vegetable garden and probably wouldn't have time to do a lot of cooking for guests.

There seemed to be many people who had moved to the country whose peace and pleasure were either spoiled or constantly threatened by the arrival of city friends who were also seeking a little peace. Everyone was complaining about this, but so far no one had found a satisfactory solution.

However, our most important reason for the guest house was the difficulty you have thoroughly enjoying something if you know people who also would get a good deal out of it if they had the chance. Fred saw this in advance more clearly than I did; through the years I have realized how true it is. When our yard is fragrant with lilacs I find myself thinking: "If only I could give Helene an armful of those!" and "Mary would love the daffodils." Later: "How Elizabeth would enjoy these tulips!"

We felt the guest house would take care of many people who ought to be breathing country air and needed a place where they could do it. Where they could write, paint, rest, wander about, enjoy themselves in their own way.

Still another advantage: they could come when they felt like it, without having to wait for an invitation to the house; they could stay a day, week, month, and bring a friend or two if there was room.

But it turned out that often, whether there was room or not, people came flocking. The place was bedlam for the first two years. It was interesting to note how differently people reacted to the idea: a few just accepted it, some exaggerated our kindness, while others considered it an insulting way to treat one's friends.

One day someone or other praised the barn arrangement to

Rex, who, knowing all we were going through at the time, replied: "Yes, it's fine. In fact it's by far the nicest *awful* idea I ever heard of."

It *was* rather awful for quite awhile in many ways, but it didn't stay awful.

That first summer on the farm Fred was there only weekends; he had some matters in New York to wind up. I moved out to stay on Saturday, March 28th, accompanied by Fred and Curly. Curly was a rather frail little Cockney whom we had hired through the League For Mutual Aid. He was about fifty years old, a panhandler when necessary, a jack-of-all-trades and good at all of them, and a character if ever there was one.

He and I were alone on the farm that first week, and I have never worked so hard in my life. For one thing, I was eager to have the place looking spic and span when Fred brought out our first guests the coming weekend; for another, Curly turned out to be a slave driver.

We ran into a snag early Monday morning: I wanted to get up early and get started, then stop at a reasonable hour, while Curly preferred to sleep late and work until all hours at night. He did manage to get up at about the time I did, because I was, after all, the boss (or at any rate the boss's wife), but he made no secret of what he thought of such a ridiculous routine, and to get even he would give me jobs which he knew I would hate. He threatened me: if I didn't give him a hand at so-and-so, he would be delayed and the place would look like a warehouse that weekend. (I *think* he said *ware*house.)

One morning he blackmailed me into shellacking the inside of the closets, and the smell made me feel dizzy; I came out to get some air. Curly gave me a disgusted look and I apologetically explained that I was going to faint. His hardboiled reception of that news shocked me into normalcy and sent me straight back into the closet.

He used every wile, that first week, to induce me to work at night, but I held out until Thursday; right after dinner, he announced that unless I helped him that evening with the livingroom floor, he couldn't possibly have it ready by the weekend.

Tentatively I asked: "What is it you want me to do?"

"Pull the tacks and nails out of the floor, so I can put the finish on it."

The livingroom had been five small rooms when we bought the house; the floor-boards, over two hundred years old, were wide and beautiful, but there were still many tacks in them which had held down the carpets through the years.

"I can't do that, Curly. I can't see well enough at night." Which was true.

"Well, you can feel, can't you?" he heartlessly replied.

Knowing when I was licked, I started the job, but Curly, having won, was satisfied and also may have felt a little sorry for me, for he growled that I was in his way and worthless besides, and sent me to bed.

He stayed all that summer. When he had finished the work he was hired to do, he remained on as a friend. We had all become attached to him, including Fred's niece, Helen, and when she and her husband moved to Montana, they took him with them. He died there some years ago.

He was a genius at moodiness; somebody would hurt his feelings and he would lie on his bed in the barn for days and refuse to eat. The guilty one would have been delighted to beg his pardon, but just try to find out who the culprit was. We would take turns offering him food and tea and finally he would break his fast; blue skies again. Poor Curly, by the end of one of those journeys into darkness, I doubt if he knew himself who had started him off.

We loved to hear him tell stories of panhandling. There is a code among these men: for instance, no gentleman would ask a man for a handout if the man was with a lady, and no gentleman panhandles in his home town.

As winter approaches they work their way to California, where they won't need an overcoat. He said that once, in Los Angeles, someone gave him a twenty-dollar bill, and one of us exclaimed: "How wonderful! Then you didn't have to pan-handle for quite awhile."

"What do you mean?" replied Curly, indignantly. "I'm no miser, I live up to my income; I had a few meals in a swell restaurant, and went to a good hotel for a night or two."

When he switched from employee to barn guest, it seemed to us that he worked harder than ever, and since we couldn't afford to pay him, we did our best to persuade him to act like a vacationist. It was true that we didn't believe in arguing with any guest who thought that mowing the lawn was good exercise and acted accordingly, yet to have Curly go on working just as he had when he was being paid was a different matter.

He pointed out that he could now do jobs if and when he pleased, with no more getting up at dawn. He was a really efficient and apparently untiring worker, and insisted he had to be busy at something. He didn't add (but we suspected it) that his diligence was prompted partly by the fact that he had no intention of deteriorating into a mere barn guest. He still ate with us; he had started out as a member of the household and refused to be demoted.

In early autumn some man (I don't remember who it was) came out for a few days and Curly instantly took such a violent dislike to him that he (Curly) left, saying (and meaning it) that if he didn't go, he would have to knock the man's block off.

That first weekend on the farm was as exciting as the open-ing day of my tearoom or as my first sight of the Russian steppe. Fred arrived late Friday afternoon with a station wagon full of friends, and more drove out on Saturday. Of course they overflowed into the house for sleeping, even onto the living-room couch.

Not only that: as mealtime approached I suddenly felt forlorn at the thought of them all going away off (a short stone's throw) to the barn to eat, so I suggested we pool our food and have it together, assuming, I suppose, that we'd also pool the labor.

But it didn't work out quite like that: it seemed that once they had deposited their food in our kitchen instead of in the barn, they felt I was the hostess, and while they wandered about on our sixty acres of woods and fields, I spent the weekend cooking for fourteen people.

Since at that time I couldn't be trusted too far in this department, it's a wonder that someone didn't offer to at least supervise, out of self-interest, but no one did. A few did take over all of the dishwashing, and excited and happy as I was about our new life, I thought that was darned nice of them.

Sunday morning Maurice and Stella Rivkin and Eve Axelrod drove in. Maurice, a doctor, had to get back to his office the following day, but Eve and Stella stayed a week.

Vladimir Koudrey also was in the barn that week. He was a tall, blond Russian, the sort of man with whom girls fall in love without any encouragement. I had met him some months previously at the home of a friend. He had walked into the room with a small paper bag in his hand. We were introduced, he bowed in stately Russian fashion and said, diffidently: "I am sorry. I love cucumbers," and took two out of the bag. "Do you love?" he asked me.

"I'm sorry, I do," I replied, and he beamed at me, handed me one, and we sat there and ate cucumbers as one eats raw apples, the way they do in Russia.

This somehow made us buddies.

When I visualize that first summer (the guest part of it, that is), it is like thinking: you know . . . that time we lived in a madhouse.

From Monday to Friday there was usually a lull. Curly of course was around, and Mother came often in the middle of the week to work on the flowerbeds, and Juanita's youngest daughter, Virginia, ten years old, came as soon as school closed and stayed all summer.

I have no talent for handling children; since Virginia and I made such a good team, I suspect *she* handled *me*. Whether we were working in the garden, or scrubbing the kitchen, or picking blueberries, or just resting on our laurels, we made a game of it, and everything we did together seemed exciting and restful at the same time.

Then came the deluge—the weekends. Fred would arrive Friday afternoon with an assortment of guests which always included Vladimir. Bess and Henry Conescu frequently drove out on Saturday. Henry is an authority on printing and Bess is an authority on every flower that grows and even those which refuse to.

Ed Carlson had given up his singing lessons and that summer was helping Rex build a house about eighteen miles from our place. Ed bought a Model T and spent many weekends with us, helping with the gigantic task of shaking dirt out of the sod in the garden and being otherwise useful.

Kay Powell came nearly every Friday in her jalopy, sometimes bringing a friend, and always her folding cot, on which she slept in the barn loft if the bedrooms were full. She wouldn't leave the cot in the barn through the week, even though I promised to defend it, for fear someone would have taken possession of it the next time she came.

Besides the regulars, people arrived in their cars, others came by train, still others hitchhiked. There were never enough beds; always an overflow into the barn livingroom, our livingroom couch, and more than once onto the haystack. People who came with the intention of spending the night stayed regardless, although I'm not saying they had a restful sleep.

One thing everyone learned early in the season: there was no use to telephone Friday night or Saturday to see if there was a vacant bed, for there never was.

Frank and Elsa Reuschle and their daughter, Parker, showed up now and then in their trailer; Frank was a retired policeman and Elsa a semi-retired chiropractor. One time they stayed several weeks, living down our back lane in the trailer.

Vladimir, who had respect for other people's privacy and a profound need for his own, built a small hut on a wooded

slope, a ten minutes' walk from our house. He called it 13 B
and slept and did some writing there, but he told me it was
primarily for my use when I needed to "go to the country
for some quiet." He built it out of old boards, furnished it with
an army cot, a chair, a gasoline stove. Everyone knew it was
there, of course, but also knew one went to 13 B by invitation
only.

That first year there wasn't even the slightest attempt on
our part to try to get it across to the barn guests that we were
merely their neighbors, not their hosts, so of course they felt
free to come into the house whenever they liked. It was quite
disconcerting to discover how often they had the urge, because
there were so *many* of them. One young woman (a friend of a
friend), overdid it a little, we thought, when she came in, went
upstairs, helped herself to my blue and silver bath-brush, returned to the yard and brushed off the seats and floor of her
little old Ford with it—not even a Buick.

It was also staggering to find how often the invitation to
use the barn was completely misinterpreted. One man whom
Fred had known since boyhood was insulted and indignant upon
receipt of his; others said they were very surprised and puzzled,
and still others seemed to feel this was just a prank on our part,
that of course they would be our guests. Usually we didn't have
the strength of character to set them right. And others seemed
to realize that they were supposed to sleep in the barn but
assumed that the rest of it—bring your own food and linen,
etc.—applied to our lesser friends, not to them.

Still others figured most peculiarly. One Friday some rather
casual acquaintances of Fred's, whom I had met only once,
drove in—a man, his wife, and their two small sons. The man
got out of the car, waving something in greeting. "We're all set!
Brought our coffeepot," he called gaily.

Since the invitation explained that the kitchen was equipped
but guests must supply their food, bringing a coffeepot was
somewhat bewildering, particularly as it turned out that they
had brought no food whatever. And no linen. It's possible they

had intended to drive to a nearby store for food, and do without sheets, but we were new to this business, so we hurriedly
made up beds in the barn for them and got it across, casually,
that we expected them to eat with us.

Then there was Loretta. I hadn't seen her for years, but
had liked her very much when we worked for some time in the
same office, so had sent her an invitation. Fred had never met
her. She wrote to ask if she could spend her vacation in the barn.

Fred went alone to the train to meet her. I told him that if
he brought back a slender, dark-haired, pretty girl (but she
must be a woman now) with beautiful merry eyes, he would
have the right one. He found her without any trouble.

Shortly after her arrival, she and I went to the barn to
select her bedroom. When I returned to the house Fred said:
"I'm sure she has no food with her; I drove her slowly past the
A & P three times but not a word out of her about wanting to
do some shopping."

Sure enough she ate with us. After she had been there a
night or two, it belatedly occurred to me that she probably
hadn't brought sheets, either, so I got some linen and took
it out to her room and began to apologize to her. Then I
glanced at her bed; it was made up neatly with the top sheet
turned back over the cover tops.

"Yes, I can still read, Ruth. The invitation said to bring
sheets."

As it turned out we loved having her eat with us. For one
thing she liked to cook and took over that job the whole time
she stayed, but more important, she had a lightness and gaiety
which should be a part of every meal; she and Fred were pals
in no time.

But we wondered: why would she bring bed linen but no
food? I think that now I understand it: the idea was too different and most people just didn't know how to proceed. We
should have been more open and helpful, should at once
have said to both the coffeepot man (I can't remember his

name) and Loretta something like this: "The best place to buy food out here is—"

The worst part of the situation was: if one friend ate with us, how would another one, preparing his own meals in the barn, feel about our apparent discrimination?

A sharp contrast to the many who misinterpreted our experiment were Bess and Henry Conescu; they entered into the spirit of it with enthusiasm, tact, and complete understanding. Henry wanted to give the barn a present of an electric refrigerator, but Bess said that with such hordes of people using the box, our bill would be staggering. Better leave it as it was, an old-fashioned box, with the guests buying ice from Mr. Banks.

The Conescus came often and if, after they returned home, a parcel-post package arrived from them, Fred or I would say: "The barn must need a pot or pan or something."

On Labor Day that year, Fred and I were to go to Edna Roth's in Norwalk for an early dinner. Around one o'clock three of our oldest friends drove in on their way home from somewhere in northern New England, and shortly after that other cars began to arrive. Some of the people had stopped just to say hello, but a number of others obviously were going to stick around for the rest of the day. Fred and I had a consultation and decided not to go off and leave them all, particularly since we knew Edna's party was a big one and we would scarcely be missed. We called her and explained the situation and she excused us but added that she, under such circumstances, would pretend she had an engagement even if she didn't, in order to get out from under.

By five o'clock we had eighteen guests, all willing to stay to dinner. We rigged up a long table in the yard and fed them chiefly on corn and tomatoes.

This seems to be an appropriate place to discuss unexpected callers, whom I am against from several angles. If I had a dollar for which I had definite plans, it is possible I might give it to you instead, if you asked for it nicely. But I'm sure

I wouldn't feel happy about it if you snatched it out of my hand. And with me it is the same with an hour, which, speaking broadly, I value more highly than I do a dollar.

If you telephoned and asked if I could spare you an hour right then, I would probably acquiesce amiably, even though it was already too full of things I wanted to do, but I would be disconcerted if you appeared without warning and helped yourself to it. Almost no one would grab money out of your hand, but many people will rob you of some of your time. An altar has been erected to the dollar bill: why don't more of us realize that another person's hour might be sacred to him?

If I don't particularly like someone, my lack of enthusiasm at his unannounced arrival needs no explanation, neither does my feeling of pleasure at the appearance of a person of whom I am fond. However, even the latter's unexpected coming is objectionable to me, for several reasons.

For one thing, I like to work by schedule, and it disturbs me to have it disrupted. Also, there are certain jobs, such as freezing or canning something, setting out plants, getting a letter in the box before the mailman comes, writing an article that has a deadline, which can't be postponed.

Of course there are a number of things you might be doing when a caller pops in, which you could continue with, but for me there are two strikes against this: first, I can't work efficiently and carry on a conversation at the same time, and second, I don't enjoy it. When I give I like to Give My All. I dislike apportioning myself, half to a caller and half to the chicken I'm preparing for dinner.

Still another bad feature: some people always look neat, even when scrubbing or doing dirty work of any kind, but I'm not that type, so when I'm in the midst of a messy job and someone arrives unexpectedly, I must make a choice: either talk to them as I am or go clean up. Taking a bath while your caller sits alone doesn't seem very hospitable, but the alternative is unappealing.

There is, however, one thing to be said for unexpected

callers. If a car you don't recognize drives in, there's a second of pleasant anticipation similar to the tingle you get when the telephone rings: now *who* is that?—even though you know that the chance of it's being someone offering you fame and fortune is one in a million. The expectancy is very brief, of course, but a thrill is a thrill and not to be despised.

CHAPTER VIII

Fish Out of Water

COLD WEATHER FORCED all barn guests to leave except Dr. Darling, an old friend who was having domestic difficulties and needed to establish a Connecticut residence.

He fixed up the kitchen for his living quarters, using the little coal-burning hot water heater for warmth. Being very tidy and handy he rigged up such a cozy nest that it was an enjoyable spot to visit. We couldn't let him have a room in the house without giving up all winter guests, and anyway it would have been an empty gesture for us to propose it, knowing he would never have consented.

Albert and Helene Hirst and their twelve-year-old son, Eric, were to be our guests on Thanksgiving; Albert was an old friend of Fred's. At that time I had seen Helene only once or twice, and knew only that she was lovely-looking, had a most attractive voice and accent (she's from Prague, Albert from Vienna) and was a marvelous cook.

I was just beginning to be hazily aware of the fact that excellent food was quite important to some people, but this hadn't yet spurred me into sparing much time and thought for this field of endeavor; it was easier to be flippant about food than to learn to cook well, and I was never at a loss for something cute to say on the subject.

It didn't bother me to serve an indifferent meal to any good cook, or to the husband of one, but it did fluster me a little when they came together. It seemed to me then (and still does) that women are unduly conscious of, and nervous about, the food their husbands eat; and I may as well confess that when Fred and I go to a friend's for dinner and discover, for instance, that the dessert is pumpkin pie (one of the few things Fred doesn't like) , I find myself feeling very sorry for him.

I had never roasted a turkey and could think of no reason to believe that even if I tried hard it would be a success, so I decided to have fried chicken for the Hirsts. At that time I hadn't learned that roasting a turkey is much simpler than frying chicken properly.

While I'm on the subject, I would like to say that although I don't expect ever to be considered an all-round first-rate cook, roast turkey is now served without embarrassment at Poverty Hollow Farm. As for fried chicken, that wonderful dish which even the best restaurants and expert home-cooks often fall down on, I will match my own against all comers.

That Thanksgiving morning I said to Fred: "If this dinner isn't the best the Hirsts have ever eaten, I can't worry about it, but I do hope they won't get here too early; if there's one thing that makes me nervous, it's a good cook around when I'm trying to do stuff."

So you can imagine how I felt when they drove in at eleven o'clock. The chicken was still in the icebox, and to tell the truth I had given very little thought as to how I would proceed with the frying of it.

I can still see Helene standing there in the kitchen, her eyes bright and cheeks pink from the frosty air. She had produced a dainty apron from her huge handbag and was now tying it around her.

"What can I do to help you?" she said, in her charming way.

Like a gift from the gods the perfect answer popped into my head: "You can't help me," I said, "but I'll be delighted to help you."

Result, a delicious dinner, but more important, our working together made Helene and me feel easy with each other for the first time. Later in the day this feeling was strengthened by another episode.

Fred and Albert went for a walk while Eric stayed with us. When he suddenly came out with a grownup remark (he was used to hearing his father discuss rather abstruse topics) I answered him. We carried on quite a lively discussion; Helene sat quietly and knitted.

When Eric went out of doors after awhile, she said to me: "You delighted him—treating him like an adult whose opinions are worth listening to."

It had pleased her, and was another step toward a friendship which has flourished ever since. She and Albert have come to our place every Thanksgiving for the past twenty-six years, and for the last seventeen, Albert's sister, Dr. Ada Elias and her husband, Dr. Herbert Elias, have also come. At one time I would have said that our original group couldn't be improved on, but Ada and Herbert have certainly added to our pleasure.

I don't think I've ever told Helene that I concentrated on talking to Eric that day because I didn't know what to say to *her*. Nor that what he said was, for the most part, over my head.

In December of that year some people (two sisters and their husbands) who had come out for a week-end in the fall with a friend of ours, and whom we had liked, wrote to ask if they might spend the New Years' weekend with us. In the house, of course. Two of them could sleep on our livingroom couch, they said, and they would bring a turkey and all the fixings and do the cooking.

Fred was willing, and I was delighted; a three-day vacation at home sounded wonderful. Unfortunately it turned out to be something rather less than that.

We had already begun to notice an interesting thing: because we lived simply, some of our guests seemed to feel they were camping out, and this appeared to sort of let down the bars to a number of them. We used no tablecloth, nor even place-mats, on our dining table; perhaps it was this that caused people to abandon even the simplest of table manners sometimes.

For instance, these four people ignored the butter knife on the plate and used their own, which I felt pretty sure they wouldn't have done in the awesome presence of a tablecloth.

Also, there are no rugs on our large livingroom floor except a rather small one in the winter for the sake of coziness, and strangely enough this seemed to make them feel that here was a place where anything was permissible; the clean couch-cushions which Fred and I sometimes used for a head-rest were tossed onto the bare floor in front of the fireplace and sat upon.

One evening when one of the girls said she was cold, I went upstairs and got my dressing gown for her: a warm, pretty garment which Rex and Fay gave me when I went to Russia. This was quite bighearted of me, for, I am sorry to say, I have a feeling against lending my clothes, except to a few people. To my pained surprise, instead of putting it on she spread it on the floor near the fire and she and her husband sat on it.

At one time during their visit, our guests decided it would be fun to play ball across the livingroom with some small pumpkins which were decorating the mantle and organ. No matter that the old Delft vases on top of the highboy or a plant or a picture might be broken; never mind that the game lasted until every pumpkin was ruined. Wasn't it obvious that, with no curtains at the windows, no tablecloth at meals, no rugs on the floor, this was a place where material possessions had no value?

And yet in our livingroom are Chinese paintings and a number of other interesting objects which Fred brought back from a trip around the world. There is a graceful curio cabinet, an attractive samovar from Russia; people do seem to like this room, with its wide floor-boards and handhewn beams two centuries old.

To complicate the puzzle of the actions of these four people and make it more baffling, we felt sure they were well-mannered enough under ordinary circumstances. And I'm not relating this episode in a spirit of criticism, although Fred and I were somewhat furious at the time. We didn't then fully grasp the meaning of their behavior.

It seems to me now that the explanation is something like this: people live largely according to rule and custom rather than ingrained esthetic feeling, and the moment you take away the environment they are used to, the rules of nice manners no longer seem to hold.

However, if any one of you who may have been tempted to live more simply is now rather discouraged for fear some of your friends will come in and wreck the place, let me quickly add that people soon adapt themselves to a departure from the norm; years ago our guests began to behave as they do in orthodox homes. So don't hesitate if you want to abandon some of the fancier things which take up your time; your friends will get used to the change, may envy you, and in time may even emulate you.

One woman we knew grasped eagerly at a chance to let go; we will call her Caroline. Wealth, social register, finishing schools were her background, and in her elegant home in New York eyebrows were raised at the slightest deviation from the Law. I can enjoy a small dose of "gracious living" if I'm not the one who has to, say, stand at the ironing-board and do the fine linen, but twenty-four hours of the strict elegance of Caroline's home was my outside limit of endurance.

It was rather a pity that I couldn't take more of it, for her establishment, with a bedroom and bath for each guest, pleasant maids, breakfast in bed, was wholeheartedly offered to Fred and me whenever we wished to go to New York for however long we cared to stay.

When Caroline first asked to come out as a barn guest, I was surprised but told her to come by all means, adding, however, that I was sure she would retreat after a day of it. But she stayed a week, and returned several times during the summer; she obviously enjoyed the experience thoroughly.

She liked to have people eat with her and often asked Fred and me, and others. Her manner of serving the meal was typical of the way she did everything while living in the barn; the hot food was brought to the table in cooking pots, so black and messy on the outside from the oil stove that it took away your appetite to have them sitting before you through the meal.

Of course there was actually nothing to criticize in Caroline's behavior; it merely seemed to reveal the fact that she lacked a sense of nicety. More than anyone I had ever known, she made me think of this from Omar Khayyam:

> What, without asking, hither hurried *Whence?*
> And, without asking, *Whither* hurried hence!
> Oh, many a cup of this forbidden Wine
> Must drown the memory of that insolence.

If ever I knew anyone who seemed to be indignant at having been born, it was poor Caroline; apparently she had been "hurried" into an environment totally unsuitable to her temperament, and it took an awful lot of messy pots to erase "the memory of that insolence."

She died a few years ago.

Now, although it is away ahead of my story chronologically, I'll tell of the bad manners of another finishing-school product. (My reason for skipping ahead is, I think, because I would like to finish, in one lump, the few unfortunate experiences we've had with guests.) A young girl (I'll call her Ellen) with a wealthy background lived not far from us, and across the road from her was the home of a farm woman of about sixty-five, whom we will call Matilda. They had no social contact although of course they knew each other.

On one or two occasions I had been present when they happened to meet and it had pained me to hear Ellen call Matilda by her first name while Matilda said "Miss Ellen." They both automatically went along with the peculiar notion that, regardless of age or anything else, Ellen, because of her money must be called "Miss," while the humble background of the older woman ruled out that little courtesy to her.

One day I was upstairs in the barn (half of which was now Fred's wood-turning shop) helping Fred select a few bowls to be sent to an art exhibit in Boston. I heard someone open the door to the shop and went out to the head of the steps to see who it was. There stood Matilda; she had come to pay a call, and getting no answer at the house, was looking for me. She was somewhat deaf so without calling down to her, I started down the steps.

At that moment Ellen opened the barn door; she too had come to see us, and when she spied Matilda, not dreaming, apparently, that a farm woman could visit socially someone whom she herself would call on, she asked:

"What do you want, Matilda?"

Gentle, modest, polite Matilda was just starting to explain when I, streaking down the steps, snapped: "She came to visit us, Ellen. What do *you* want?"

Instantly I was sorry for my manner. When we were growing up, Mother gave us very few rules to live by; she was a Quaker and followed her own Inner Light, encouraging us, as far as possible, to do the same. But she used to say this: "Never praise or blame anyone, including yourself," and I agree with this, theoretically. Our emotions are another story, but one look at Ellen's puzzled face was enough to cool my wrath.

The difficulty was that her training and education had taught her how to behave only among her "equals"; she hadn't enough innate sensitivity to know how to act when someone on her accepted level received an "inferior" socially. However, please don't get the idea that I believe finishing schools turn out only ill-mannered products; there must be a number of girls who have good enough stuff in them to come through almost unharmed. But I'm not at all sure that if I had a daughter I would be courageous enough to put her to the test.

Our second summer was more hectic than the first, if that's possible. The depression was bearing down heavily now, and of course there were many people who needed a vacation and couldn't afford one. The barn was constantly full to overflowing. Many hitchhiked from New York.

My niece, Virginia, was again with us all summer and every summer after that until she got married. Now and then she would have a friend out for a few days and they would do their own cooking in the barn. Virginia was eleven now, and the first time she planned to do this, her mother said to her: "I'm sure you'll make out all right but that oil range worries me a little; promise me that you'll always ask Ruth or Fred to light it for you."

"Of course, Mother," replied Virginia, a twinkle in her expressive grey eyes, "but is it all right if I still light it for the other people in the barn? They're all afraid to. I light Ruth's, too; I'm better at it than she is."

Vladimir, who wasn't very well, also spent the summer with us. He slept at 13 B but had his meals with us, and I suggested to him and Fred that they each take a turn at getting dinner once a week. They agreed to this, but Fred was so scientific that he made too big a job of it, and Vladimir invariably needed about seven things I had never heard of. Virginia pointed out to me that the only time I was completely exhausted was on the nights they did the cooking, which was true, so I went back to a seven-day week.

When Vladimir felt morose, he consciously or unconsciously dressed to suit his mood, and wandered about in dark colors, looking exactly like Hamlet. Even not counting the clothes and the melancholy, he actually did resemble Hamlet on these occasions. One day when he was bathed in gloom, he asked if anyone was going to Bethel, a village seven miles away; Fred told him that if arsenic was what he wanted, there was some in the tool shed.

Vladimir replied: "I want nothing. Just wish to go for a trip. Time was I would go to some foreign country when I felt restless; now I am happy if I may go to Bethel."

I must have come into some fortune or other which has slipped my mind, for I bought some lumber for Vladimir to add another room to 13 B. The one tiny original room was made more or less of kindling and was threatening to collapse at any moment.

The hut being situated where it was, the lumber, when

delivered, had to be dumped quite a distance away, so it became a matter of courtesy for anyone who was asked to 13 B to stop and pick up one of the new boards and carry it through the blueberry patch, across a tiny stream and up the hill to the hut.

Vladimir dictated a novel to me that summer; that is, together we translated into English a novel which he had written in Russian. His style was so charming and individualistic that, although his English was inadequate, I hesitated to suggest a single word, and often I had him say a sentence perhaps twenty times or more until it was correct English—his, though, not mine.

That second year of gardening I worked very hard but wasn't outstandingly successful; one day someone chided Vladimir for taking up so much of my time with his novel and he answered: "Much better that she sits up at 13 B in the shade than to be in the garden in the sun watching a carrot not get bigger."

For twenty-seven summers Dominick Mercurio has driven into our yard on Tuesdays and Fridays in his truck; he sells fruit and vegetables. I buy fruit from him and once in a long time a vegetable; for several years he bought vegetables from me. The barn guests have spent many a dollar on his products.

One day Fred stepped out into the yard and saw Dominick sitting on his runningboard eating a banana; Fred asked him if that was the extent of his lunch and Dominick said yes. We were just about to sit down to lunch and Fred persuaded him to come in and eat with us; after that he often had lunch with us when he arrived at the right time.

Fred and I feel it's presumptuous to address a man by his first name merely because he drives a vegetable wagon, while he says Mister and Missus to us; before long Fred had Dominick calling him Fred. Calling me Ruth seemed to come a little harder to him, and for some time he settled for "Ruth, ma'am." For many years now, though, he has skipped the "ma'am."

Dominick had often told us that someday he would cook us a real Italian meal, and finally, a Sunday in late August was decided on. The Conescus, who were coming out that weekend, were included in the invitation.

The food was to be prepared at our place, so around noon on the day chosen Dominick showed up with his wife, mother-in-law, three children, all the makings for the dinner and several huge pots and pans. Three things stand out in my mind regarding that party: the dinner was just wonderful, the mother-in-law and I fell in love with each other (she spoke only a little English and I no Italian, so we sat and beamed at each other), and the three-year-old child in his immaculate white suit got into a pan of crankcase drainings and was soon black from head to foot.

During that second winter, Dr. Darling's son, Bill, stayed with us in the house for some time; he was a very appealing young man. I say "was" because he has gone out of our lives; his father died years ago and shortly afterward Bill moved to California. At that time Bill was at loose ends and his father thought that perhaps Fred could give him some help psychologically.

Once when I returned from a few days in New York, I discovered that the men had scrubbed the kitchen floor in honor of my homecoming. Newspapers had been spread around to protect the floor, and when I started to pick them up the next morning Bill said: "Just a minute, Ruth; I want those in the corner by the stove," and he hurried over and rescued them.

It seemed that someone had given Fred a batch of old papers, and after he and Bill had covered the floor with them, they saw big headlines screaming at them under their feet; the newspapers were copies of the Bridgeport scandal sheet and the tales they had to tell were intimate and naughty. The two men claimed they had spent hours crawling around on hands and knees, catching up on the latest; Bill had finished all of them except the ones around the stove.

Aside from the racy stories, the men, although living in the country where city folks think absolutely nothing ever happens, had more interesting things to relate than I did, fresh from the biggest town in the world. Fred told about the man he had picked up in the car near Bethel; he was a machinist, in his middle forties, out of a job and broke. (The depression was still going strong.)

This man had hitchhiked from Jersey and said he was headed for the police station in Bridgeport, where he thought he would be allowed to spend the night; he had hopes of a job in Bridgeport. Fred told him he could spend the night at our place, and after they got to the house, Fred said he had an engagement for dinner, told the man where to sleep, showed him where the food was, and told him to cook himself a meal. The man seemed surprised that he was to be left alone on the place. (Bill had gone to New Rochelle for the night.)

Fred went upstairs to take a shower, and when he came down, there was his new friend in his shirtsleeves having some coffee before the open fire, reading a magazine.

The next morning, after a hearty breakfast, Fred drove him to Bridgeport.

Of course the story, to have an interesting climax, should end with the man robbing us right and left, and a moral: never trust anyone. Or, much better, he should have been an eccentric millionaire in disguise and have sent Fred a substantial check. Moral: trust everyone and some day it may pay off.

But the dull truth is that he didn't steal a thing, and no check has as yet shown up. He must have been just as represented: an honest machinist down on his luck.

Bill's news was that Fred had taken a woman to the movies while I was away, but when he told me who it was and I recalled her weight, I merely smiled indulgently. Not that there isn't many an attractive woman here and there in whose presence it isn't tactful to mention poundage, but they aren't Fred's type. That is, *then* they weren't; at present almost his favorite person is Marjorie Foley, who is full of good resolutions about reducing.

Vladimir used to say: "I believe I go West where men are men and Vladimir is nothing." That next spring he did go to California. A few years later, he died. This was a sad thing for me. He was about the age of Donald, and I had, in a way, mothered him as I had Donald. It was hard to lose both of them.

CHAPTER IX

God Blesses Our Home
But He Doesn't Sweep It

SPRING AGAIN, our third in Poverty Hollow, and on May Day Isabel Turner and my sister Elizabeth went with me to the garden to cut asparagus. I was glad for their company; gathering your own asparagus for the very first time is somewhat of a performance and calls for an audience. In their seeming intelligence all things that grow are fascinating to me, and the tender stalks of asparagus appear to have unusual energy and even courage, as they push their way through so much firm earth in their determination to reach the light.

Elizabeth and Isabel also appreciate the miracles around them in a growing garden and love to work in it. The out-of-doors activities of most of the barn guests were confined to lying on their backs in the sun, getting a luxury tan, and taking long walks.

That summer was another hectic one. At one time there were twenty-two people, counting all of us, on the place for a stretch of a few weeks. With only eight single beds available to the barn guests, perhaps you're wondering where all of them slept. There is a 25 x 50 loft, and various guests brought out cots and put them up there. Now and then a few unfortunates were obliged to sleep on blankets on the floor.

My father died. Mother had a cottage built on our property, not far from the house, and for several years she and Mary lived there for about eight months of the year. They had privacy of a sort, but one day Mary said she was thinking of going back to 42nd Street and Broadway, for a little peace and quiet.

Ed Carlson had gone home to Colorado, Vladimir was in

California, Curly was no longer around, and a few of the others who had been in evidence a lot that first year or two came less often now. But of course there were dozens of others to take their places, and 13 B came in most handy. I often went there to get away from it all.

Fred had a bugle on which he blew different calls for me if I was at the hut when visitors arrived. Or, rather, since bugles have so few notes, he paraphrased some tunes. *Home Sweet Home* meant: "Some people you like have arrived. Come home." *Woman is Fickle* meant (and most unjustly) : "People have come, but you're so changeable that I'm not sure whether you still like them or not." The third one was *Cucaracha* (cockroach) : his meaning in that case is obvious.

Naturally the visitors, particularly the third group, were kept in ignorance of the significance of the tune he played; he would merely say: "I'll blow the bugle; if Ruth is within hearing, she'll come." I do hope that no one for whom he played *Cucaracha* will read this.

For self-protection almost no one was asked to 13 B; Edmund Barach was one of the exceptions. We met him through our old friend, Joseph Gollomb, who stayed in the barn for awhile in April while finishing his book *Unquiet.*

Edmund is the brother of Dr. Alvin Barach who invented the oxygen tent. Edmund had studied dentistry, practiced for a short time, and then abandoned the profession because he found it distasteful. For one thing, he claimed that many people ate onions immediately before a visit to the dentist. When we met him he had just gone into the oxygen tent business.

He had a gift for writing but not much experience; at his request I undertook to go over with him some stories he had written. As with Vladimir, I was careful not to suggest phrases or even words, for he too had an original style which I didn't want to spoil.

He had difficulty (which, as a matter of fact, I also have) in taking care of the most ordinary events in a story; for instance, if his characters were, say, on the lawn in a tense situation of some kind, he had no trouble handling their emotions and dialogue, but if they were then supposed to go into the house, he had trouble getting them there.

When he was in New York, he often sent me manuscripts to read and criticize. Once he sent a story about two old ladies who lived in Vermont; it was essential that they take a trip to Baltimore. Knowing my disinclination to compose a sentence or even add a word to his stories, he attempted to bribe me. He wrote: "Ruth: I don't know what the fare is from Manchester to Baltimore but I'll find out and send it to you if you'll only get these two old gals down there for me."

It's a little humiliating, but the only story he sold was one I didn't tamper with.

During the blizzard of 1934 we were snowed in for a week and Edmund telephoned from New York to ask if we needed food. I'm sure he was disappointed when Fred told him we had plenty. He was used to sending oxygen tents out by plane for all sorts of emergencies and no doubt was hoping we were starving so that he could have some groceries dropped on our doorstep.

When Phyllis Comara bought an acre or two from us at the extreme end of our property and began to build on it, she spent every weekend in the barn, in order to supervise her project. She usually brought her two sons and several friends with her.

Phyllis is the sister of Lawrence Langner of the Theatre Guild. The Comara is short for Comaraswami, which is the name of the Hindu she married in London when she was sixteen. Their sons were born in India. Phyllis got a divorce from the Hindu, married a second time, was again divorced; at this time she was sort of playing the field.

Being energetic, generous, and expansive, every Saturday night she invited everyone on our place to dinner; she was an excellent cook. On top of everything else, she was attractive and a born flirt. (What an old-fashioned and inadequate word that is for it!)

Fred came in for a share of her attentions, and once I asked her if I would have to return all the presents she had given me when she found out she couldn't take him away from me. Her brown eyes twinkling, she replied: "Oh, no. You're in a separate compartment."

One day in September of our fourth year on the farm, Fred said to me: "I don't believe we've had one single evening of privacy since May."

This shocked us into taking steps, and the following spring the barn guests found a few rules tacked up on the walls, the most important one being that the barn dwellers would please be good enough to consider themselves our neighbors, not our guests, and to come to the house by invitation only.

There was already a so-called rule on the wall in the hall regarding the cleaning of the barn; Fred had commissioned a friend to embroider a handsome cross-stitched motto which read:

> God Blesses Our Home
> But He Doesn't Sweep It.

This amused the guests but I can't say it accomplished anything further. Most of them, before departing, superficially cleaned the bedrooms they had occupied, but the neutral ground (halls, kitchen, washroom) was usually left for the other fellow to do. The only trouble with that was that the other fellow was no dope either.

(Each spring and fall I gave the barn a thorough cleaning and aired the blankets and mattresses.)

We were surprised, although I don't suppose we should have been, when some people's feelings were hurt by the rule which demoted them to neighbors. Joe Gollomb was the first one; he came out in April to work on a novel.

Joe was an old friend of mine; we had canoed together at Camp Tamiment, had sat in Village tearooms trading dreams, had seen Chartres together when I met him in Paris on my way home from Russia. (When we entered the cathedral he put a handkerchief on my head; I had abandoned hats long before the twenties.) Joe, too, had got me neatly out of trouble at a small dinner party in a restaurant in Paris, when, faced with my first artichoke, I hadn't a notion of how to deal with it.

Now, staying in the barn, his feelings were hurt because he didn't have free access to the house; he didn't expect to eat with us but he didn't see why, having finished his dinner, he couldn't bring over a bottle of wine and share it with us at our evening meal.

Fred did his best to explain: "We've had open house for nearly six months of the year, Joe, and it's been like living in an institution where you don't get away from people except when you're in the bathroom. It's just got to be too much of a good thing."

"But I should think that with old friends . . ." protested Joe.

"If you were the only person in the barn right now it would be different," I said, "but Bud Palmer, who is also over there, has known Fred longer than I have you, and we're very fond of *him* too. It's always something like that."

Joe was unable to accept our explanation, even though we went on to say that in a setup such as this was, casual acquaintances and even strangers whom somebody may have sent to the barn for a needed vacation would feel slighted and left out of it if some of our friends, also staying in the barn, were allowed special privileges in the house. But we were careful not to hurt him still more by adding that even from real friends, one or more of whom was usually in the barn, we needed a respite now and then during our leisure time.

When Bess and Henry Conescu first saw the rules, Henry, too, was insulted. They came out for a weekend, and although Henry didn't say anything, we knew he was hurt because he avoided the house so meticulously.

During weekends it was understood that our livingroom was open to everyone at any time, and Saturday and Sunday evenings the whole crowd gathered there. That Sunday, in the late afternoon, I was on the upstairs porch which overlooks our kitchen door, and I heard someone knocking on it. Glancing down, I saw it was Henry carrying a tray which contained four cocktails; I called to him to go on in and ran downstairs to greet him. Bess showed up shortly and we called Fred.

"On the Sabbath, when you know everyone's welcome, and when you come bearing gifts, you knocked. Why did you do that, Henry?"

Of course I knew why, but both Fred and I had been wanting to discuss our problems with the Conescus and this seemed a good opening.

"I didn't want to intrude," he replied, his eyes fastened on the glass in his hand.

Just then someone came into the room—an example of how difficult it was to have a private conversation with anyone. Henry and Bess stayed only a few minutes longer, then wandered out. Half an hour later I spied them sitting in the yard alone and Fred and I went out and joined them.

I said: "You and Bess have been really wonderful about this whole barn business, Henry, and we won't be able to bear it if you're going to be hurt and get disgusted with the whole thing. It was ridiculous for you to knock at the door today. Why did you?"

"It's those rules you've put up. I *hate* rules," replied Henry, gloomily.

"So do we," Fred agreed, "but when we woke up to the fact, one day last September, that we hadn't had one single evening to ourselves for several months, we spent some time during the winter trying to solve the problem and the only solution we could come up with was to put up some rules. The unfortunate part is that rules under these circumstances must apply alike to close friends and to strangers, even though we don't even like the strangers much."

Henry grunted; Bess looked unhappy.

"This whole thing is an unprecedented situation for us as well as for everyone else involved," I said, "and no doubt we ourselves have made plenty of mistakes. We need advice. What would you do, Henry?"

He exploded: "Me? Ha! I'd have burned the damn barn down long ago."

"Go ahead, it's insured," replied Fred encouragingly.

And this cleared the atmosphere even though it didn't solve the problem.

A year or two later we took down the rules; they were no longer necessary. For the stumbling block hadn't been lack of consideration; it had been, merely, that the majority of barn guests made a relatively short stay and enjoyed a "get-together" in the evenings. It wasn't surprising that they didn't realize we were getting an overdose of sociability.

It is perhaps superfluous to add that the few people who stayed for weeks at a time had, oftener than not, spent the evenings in their rooms.

CHAPTER X

Pre-Sputnik Sputnik

SUSAN TOWNSEND, an artist, and a friend from my Village days, moved into the barn loft for the summer, and did some painting up there. We were now trying to hold the number of guests down to eight at a time, which had been our original intention, but we weren't having much luck; they sometimes slept two in a single bed and overflowed into the barn livingroom. We didn't let anyone invade Susan's loft, though.

The barn was settling down to a new pattern; the weekenders were fewer because the bedrooms were often occupied by people who were staying a longer time. A number came for several weeks' vacation.

One day, out of a clear sky, I got bighearted and wrote to a liberal organization in New York, asking if they would like to have us run a benefit for them, a clambake. They naturally replied they would be delighted, and from that moment our troubles began. We had three of these affairs for successive summers and made money for the organization and some new friends for ourselves.

Oscar and Joan Schapira are two of these friends. We were buying green coffee from the Schapira Coffee Co. in New York and roasted it two or three times a week, but realizing it would be much too big a job to roast enough for one hundred people, Fred wrote the company, telling them about the clambake, and asking if they would send us enough freshly roasted coffee for it. He also asked how to make that amount.

In reply he received a letter from David Schapira saying that he and his brother Oscar and their wives would like to buy tickets for the party, that they would send the coffee to us the day before, and would come early the next day and make it.

We were so pleased by their co-operation that we sent them a barn invitation suggesting they spend the night before the clambake in the barn. That was reckless, because there was sure to be an overflow of people around on that Saturday to help with the party and naturally they would spend the night in the barn.

There is a large, gently-sloping depression in our meadow which is a perfect spot for hanging a steam kettle, and luckily enough we had a huge iron one which our predecessors had used for scalding pigs. Two of our neighbors, Matt and John Lorenz, volunteered to do the job of rigging up a tripod for the kettle, and also offered to take full charge of the fire and the steaming.

We borrowed long tables and benches which we placed on the level ground in the meadow between the clam pot and the vegetable garden. We bought clams, frankfurters, rolls, butter, cream, and sugar, but all the cakes were donated, and the garden supplied corn, tomatoes, and cabbage for cole-slaw which Mother made.

Naturally there were a few minor mishaps. When they are turned out to pasture, city dwellers can't be expected to operate without some blunders. Fred caught one offender just in time: he had come up on Saturday to "help" and when several of them finished washing a tubful of clams, he made for our well and was starting to dump the dirty water into it when Fred saw him. He evidently thought wells were oversized slop-pails.

Charlotte Lorenz, John's sister, was a godsend, with her efficiency and good humor, and two of our other neighbors (wealthy invaders, not natives) tried to outdo each other with contributions: flowers, cakes, a baked ham in case the food ran short.

These were churchgoing women who had set out to snub us a few years before, when we moved to the neighborhood. I'm sure they felt justified, with our barn occupied by such an undiscriminating assortment of God's children. "Foreigners of *every* sort, my dear, and *Negroes*, I'm positive!"

The story of how these neighbors were determined to put us in our place and keep us there, how they failed because we liked our place and stayed in it of our own accord, is pathetic because snobbery of every kind has pathos. But it was amusing, too; our indifference to their attitude was too much for their curiosity. They simply had to investigate, and to everyone's surprise we all liked each other.

It was of course a satisfaction that the clambake was a success, but the best thing that happened to us through it was Neil Lowenthal. He was at the head of the organization for which the party was given, and we hadn't met him before, but almost at once a friendship sprang up between him, Fred, and me. Neil was in his late twenties; idealistic, intelligent, earnest, but his lively sense of humor prevented him from taking himself too seriously.

Neil had offered the very considerable fortune his father had left him to some radical organization, but they had refused to take the bulk of it, saying it would be of more value if he kept the money to live on and donated his time to them. I don't know specifically what organization that was, but even if it was *you-know-what*, let him who has wholeheartedly offered his fortune, *all* of it, to something he believes in, make the first comment.

Neil worked too hard, as most people do who labor for an ideal; we persuaded him, that Sunday after the first clambake, to stay over for a day or two. Then hearing, a short time later, that he was really overdoing it and headed for a breakdown, Fred wrote and urged him to be our house guest for awhile and get some rest.

Neil's answer was full of amazement at such kindness—opening our home to any tired person, even one who was almost a stranger—but Fred sent him an immediate reply saying our invitation was more flattering to him than to us, and that he

would please not tell the whole liberal movement that when
they were in need of a rest they could have an indefinite one
with the Rossiters.

Our invitation was for him alone, Fred said, and had been
extended because we had discovered, even in that one short
visit with us, he could become a member of our household
without disrupting it in the least. Neil came, and that was the
beginning of a lasting friendship.

The following June, a friend of Susan's from Westport drove
over to see her one day. Susan was again spending the summer
in the barn loft. We all had tea together and as usual when
anyone visited the barn for the first time, there was some discussion about it.

I said that what I would like was a Russian who spoke no
English to spend the summer in the barn, then I wouldn't
forget the little Russian I knew. Susan's friend replied that
if I was serious she thought she could supply me with two
Russians.

She told us about Arkady and Masha Bessmertny; Masha
was an actress and a dancer and had come to the United States
with the *Moscow Art Theater,* and her husband had come,
too. The theater engagement was over, but they wanted to stay
in America for a few months. They had very little money.
Arkady, who was badly crippled from infantile paralysis, was
a sculptor.

I said to send them along by all means, if they cared to come.
They wouldn't get to see much of America, and what they
would see wouldn't be strictly typical, but we could guarantee
that they wouldn't be lonesome.

They arrived early in July and stayed until the middle
of October. Unfortunately for me they, like all the Russians
I have ever known, mastered twenty English words while I was
mastering one in Russian. And they were so eager to learn
English that I hadn't the heart to talk Russian with them at all.

They occupied a room in the barn just big enough to hold

two single beds, a dresser and a chair; the space between the beds can't be more than three feet, and yet Masha (I just don't know how on earth she accomplished it) managed to make that tiny crowded room inviting, if not actually attractive.

Arkady had a wonderfully soothing effect on me and sometimes, when barn guests were swarming and buzzing around and showing no mercy, I would escape to this little room. Masha would insist that I stretch out on her bed, putting my feet on a newspaper, and if anyone rapped on the door and asked if I was there, she would fire "No" at them in four languages—*Nyet, No, Non, Nein*—while Arkady was swearing at them under his breath in Russian.

He spent far too much energy being annoyed at the barn guests; he felt that most of them harrassed and imposed on us. Masha spent too much time being indignant because they didn't leave the barn cleaner when they departed.

She would condole with me and I would reply: "I know they don't leave it as they should, Masha, but what can I do?"

"Write. Not come again, say."

"Oh, *nyevozmozhna!*" I would tell her. (I did manage to get in a Russian word once in awhile. That one means "impossible.")

One day she asked me: "How you say *sveen?*"

"Pig," I told her.

"Peeg! Peeg!" she cried angrily, in reference to some recently departed guest. Then: "I clean. Not for they. For you."

I hadn't been able to make her see that it didn't do *me* any good for her to diligently clean after everybody, and even if she had understood, it wouldn't have made any difference. She had to clean, not for me as I'm sure she believed, but for her own peace of mind; a dirty room made her unhappy.

As a matter of fact she more than once indignantly showed me one of the bedrooms which seemed to me to have been left in fine shape. However, I was careful not to let her discover how low my own standards were; that I was somewhat of a peeg myself by *her* standards.

Arkady borrowed one end of Susan's loft and I posed for him; he made a head of me, which is still out in the barn gathering dust, and still looking like me in my crossest mood. Masha said he shouldn't have made it while I had a clambake (this was the second one) on my mind.

Lora Baxter and Dick Kelly, who worked in Neil's office, came out a few days before the Sunday of the clambake; this one turned out to be bigger and more successful financially than the first one, and after it was over, Lora remained in the barn for a vacation. This was her first visit to our place.

She was an efficient, attractive girl, with red hair and greenish eyes. After she had been a barn guest for a few days she came over to the house one day, out onto the porch where Fred and I were having lunch.

"This is out of order, I know, barging in on you," she began, "but I have something important to say, so perhaps you'll forgive me. I was so tired when I came out here that I've done nothing but sit around in the yard, and I can hardly believe what I've seen going on. You are intelligent people and yet I don't think you have any idea of what you've gotten your-selves into; I'm amazed at you."

Fred asked her what she meant and she gladly went on; she was full and running over with it.

"Well, for instance, every morning when Ruth starts out to the garden after breakfast, she's delayed over and over; the first day I was here five people (and there may have been others before I started to count) stopped her and asked her to do something or other, and the second morning there were seven, this morning, six. She's asked to order eggs, give a message to the milkman, order some ice, take an order for Dominick in case they're having a nap or out for a walk when he comes, and heaven knows what else. And as busy as you are, Ruth, you meekly obey, waiting on people who have nothing to do all day but take care of these things for themselves."

"I know, and I've told her dozens of times . . ." Fred began but Lora interrupted.

"Hold it. You'd better begin to tell yourself a few things. This morning it took you nearly an hour to get into your workshop, which is less than a minute's walk across the yard, what with various questions and requests from barn guests."

We tried to justify some of these goings-on; for instance, we told her we preferred to call the egg and the ice man ourselves, rather than have people running into the house at any and all hours to do their own telephoning.

Lora said: "All right, but why don't you choose a certain time, convenient for you, for people to present their demands for the next twenty-four hours? If anyone forgets something, let him do without it. Let me arrange it; I'll be here another week and I'll have anyone's life who asks for something out of turn."

"Then you'll go home, and new people will come, and it's embarrassing to act as though our time was so sacred," I replied hesitantly.

"I'll leave, yes, but Arkady will be here; I've talked to him about this. He fairly boils at the thought of the demands made on you busy people. He's bursting to take over when I go."

Well, it worked like a charm from the first. Lora pointed out to everybody that if you multiply one trifling request by twelve, the answer isn't so trifling. They all entered in. They had just forgotten that little drops of water make a mighty ocean.

In this barn experiment, I'm sure Fred and I made as many mistakes as the guests did; it was new to all of us. But it's interesting, and significant, I think, that through the years the guests, accustomed to the idea, if not the practice, of communal living, co-operated with each other with scarcely a hitch. A good many different kinds of people had to share one kitchen, one washroom, one shower, one toilet, and if there was any real unpleasantness at any time it didn't reach *our* ears.

On the other hand, the relation between the guests and us was a new one, and it took time to iron out the wrinkles.

CHAPTER XI

The Bank Fails

I'M SORRY FOR SNOBS; it seems to me that our lives are narrow and petty enough without our deliberately making them more so. This pitfall of snobbery is one I have mercifully escaped. For instance, although I find that wealthy people are all cut from the same limited pattern, I can have a cup of tea with a multimillionaire, whose whole life has been one of luxury, without the slightest feeling of condescension. He's a victim of his environment and what little there is to him may be fine. But I'm realistic about him: I just don't expect very much. For help in any situation which takes something more than an adequate bank account to solve (such as running a clambake, for instance), don't give me a person who has never been *obliged* to earn his bread and butter, his place in the world.

The third and last clambake was financially a big success but too many headaches to be worth the work and worry. Neil was no longer in charge of the organization and the man who had taken his place (we'll call him Putnam) was the very wealthy son of a very wealthy father.

He was, I think, an intelligent and considerate man, and wanted to do everything he could to make the affair a success. He sent two of his gardeners over to our place one morning, a day or two before the clambake, to . . . well, I really can't tell you what they were supposed to do and they certainly didn't know either. I was too busy to bother with them; Mother entertained them. She took them on a tour of our vegetable and flower gardens, gave them some cuttings, and I wouldn't be surprised if she persuaded them to spade up a new flower bed or two for her.

As more and more tickets were sold in advance, and we had to scout around for more tables and chairs, order more food, and so on, I got a little panicky and began to send urgent letters to Dick Kelly in New York saying we needed help of one kind and another; all the satisfaction I got was a series of long-distance telephone calls, telling me to be calm, to stop worrying. As I hung up one day after one of these, it occurred to me that there wasn't much point in our turning ourselves inside out in the effort to make money for the organization if they were going to spend it all in an effort to keep me calm.

On the Wednesday before the clambake, two girls and a man came out to lend a hand, and stayed in the barn the rest of the week. They were strangers to me. Jean Pratt, one of the girls, who worked in the office of the organization and the man (her husband) were a real help, but the other girl had brought her violin and seemed to need to practice about sixteen hours a day.

Jean told me that when my rather frantic letters kept arriving, she had tried to get Dick to do something constructive about my appeals but he would merely say: "Relax. Ruth always goes into a spin before the shindig but they come off as smooth as glass."

Another girl, Eva Wentz, came out on Thursday, and Dick arrived Friday morning. He's very likable, intelligent, has a nice sense of humor but, unfortunately for my needs that particular weekend, he's endowed with the artistic temperament.

Jean and her husband continued to be very helpful but the violinist was faithful to her ART and Eva and Dick were usually off on a long walk, lapping up the country air. I found myself getting pretty annoyed with them.

Saturday afternoon I discovered that the long grass under the big old appletree on the edge of the meadow, where the tables were to be placed, was full of rotting apples, and I realized it would be quite a job to get rid of them.

I shouldn't be put in a position where I'm forced to try to make people do something they don't want to; I'm no good at it. I don't like it, but in this instance I had no choice. I called Dick, showed him the apples, and said: "Everyone of them has to be cleaned out of there; if people get rotten apple stains on their clothes, they're going to be annoyed."

He went to get the other helpers, and soon they all showed up. All but the violinist, that is. We got the wheelbarrow and some rakes and started in, but I saw that the grass was too long for us to get anywhere with rakes.

"This is no good," I said. "We're only making a worse mess in the grass. We'll have to pick each apple up one by one," and I leaned over and tried to get hold of a couple; they squashed in my fingers.

"That way . . . with our hands?" exclaimed Dick, wrinkling his nose in distaste.

"I hope you'll never have to face anything worse than picking up some rotten apples," I cuttingly replied.

I think that was the moment he and Eva realized I was disgusted with them and they fell to with a vengeance. We were making good headway when it began to rain; without a word I went on working and so did the rest. I was thinking: they're subdued for the moment and we'll just have to finish the job while they're squelched. I'd certainly hate to have to get mad at them all over again.

Shortly the musician called from the barn window: "Why don't you all come in? It's raining."

Dick yelled back: "No it isn't. It won't be raining until Ruth says it is."

A good laugh was had by all. I said it was raining and we quit. The next morning they finished the job without my having to mention it.

There were over two hundred guests at this final clambake. Putnam arrived late; he hurried up to me and apologized, explaining that he had had to finish a game of croquet with some movie actress (I don't recall her name). She was spending the weekend at his place, so he had brought her along. At that very busy time, with a few dozen things on my mind, he expected me to take time out to meet her and be social and gracious.

Putnam was at the head of this organization for which quite a number of us were working our heads off, but not for a second, apparently, did it occur to him to ask if there wasn't something he could do. I'm fairly sure he wouldn't have considered it beneath him to wait on a table, for instance; the idea itself was simply beyond him. He was a nice person, too, and possibly even competent in, well, a croquet game, let us say.

How then can his behavior be explained except by the fact that never having *had* to do anything constructive in his whole life for anyone, including himself, he was still a two-year-old in that one large, important department?

Is someone protesting that he knows rich people who would have pitched in and helped? So do I. Then why all this talk about Putnam's wealth? Because I think that in his case too much money had made him useless; it's unimportant that he was a total loss at the clambake, but I'm afraid he was useless in general, and if you're of no use you must be wishy-washy, and if so, can you possibly be happy? I'm sorry for Putnam; that's the long and short of it.

Seven years passed, during which the clientele in the barn changed, more or less constantly. Some of the earlier guests moved to far cities, some acquired homes of their own in the country, the W.P.A. kept many artists and writers busy, with little free time. Also, many, as the depression receded, could afford vacations where they didn't have to cook for themselves.

Most of our guests had always agreed on one thing: they wanted us to charge something for the use of the barn. Knowing that we lived on a small income, they wanted to relieve us of the barn expenses, such as oil for the cook stove, electricity, and so on. The things which really mounted up—repairs on the floors of bedrooms, hall and kitchen, copper pipes in place of the iron ones, a new septic tank—they were not aware of.

We disliked the idea of accepting any payment; if it amounted to enough to cover our costs, it would change the

whole atmosphere of the place. Also, it might put us under
certain obligations: if we made a charge, people might feel
they could complain, and make demands. Too, it wouldn't
surprise me if one reason for our objection was that we were
enjoying the role of bighearted givers.

We had hoped that the barn would become a unit, practically apart from us, that when a new blanket was needed,
or pots were burned, or anything was broken, the guests would
take care of it. Bess and Henry had always done that, but they
had a place on Long Island now, and were more likely to visit
us in the house in the winter than to come out in the summer,
although they did drive out now and then just for the day. And
of course we didn't want the burden to fall on one or two
people.

If everyone hadn't done so much talking about wanting to
pay, I think we would hardly have noticed the lightheartedness
with which they threw away broken dishes and burned pots
with never a replacement. When the garbage pail wore out,
we purposely didn't get another for a while, curious to see if
any of them would. No one did.

Harry and Julie Kohn, who came every summer for a
month's stay until they bought a place of their own, did everyone a valuable service when they had the barn livingroom
screened. It was upstairs now, part of Susan's loft, for Fred
had turned more than half of the barn into a shop, where he
was making bowls, platters, salad-servers, all sorts of things in
wood. It was a blessing to us as well as the guests to have that
room screened; it had been somewhat disquieting to sit on our
own protected porch and hear our friends slapping mosquitoes
in the yard.

Harry was also Mother's Good Man Friday; sweet-natured
and obliging, he was always ready to do some digging or haul-
ing for her.

Looking back, it's fairly clear what the trouble was regarding
the upkeep of the barn. If the guests had all been paying a

certain amount, they would no doubt have felt that was a fair arrangement—everyone was doing an equal share. But as things were, they probably figured: Why should I replace dishes, or the garbage pail, or get some new pots for everyone to use and abuse?

We made a mistake in not saying frankly what was in our minds: we don't want to charge you people, but why don't you get together and figure out a way to keep the barn from running down? It's *your* place; why don't you take care of it?

In the spring of the eighth year, someone (we never did find out who) put a bank in the barn kitchen with a typewritten note tacked up over it, which read something like this:

We all keep saying we want to help with the expense of the barn upkeep. Here's your chance. Do it NOW!

We were pleased at this. Without our having to make the suggestion, they had taken over the responsibility.

Well, I doubt if the most cynical of you will guess what happened. It's true the barn was less crowded now; we didn't let anyone else come if the bedrooms were filled, and there was no longer a loft to take care of an overflow. This meant there were never more than eight guests accommodated at one time. However, if each person had dropped ten cents into the bank for each night he spent in the barn that summer, there would have been about ninety dollars in it at the end of the season. There was exactly one dollar and fifty-five cents.

The reason for this may have been something like the following: most of the guests more or less unconsciously assumed that the others were putting something in the bank; why should they, since no one would give them credit if they did, or know it if they didn't? It was just everyone's hard luck that so little was contributed that it made all of them look small.

Our first feeling when we opened the bank was astonishment, then some indignation, and finally tolerance. It wasn't hard to think up excuses: this one forgot, that one was broke, intended to leave something the next time and didn't get to come again. And so on.

Wistfully we figured that five cents a night wouldn't have been a strain on anyone, and would have netted us nearly fifty dollars with which to brighten up the barn a bit. However, probably no one could contribute only a nickel without feeling small; oddly enough, putting in nothing at all would probably seem less petty.

We removed the bank, and since it had failed, one might suppose that the plea to persuade us to make a regular charge for using the barn would then die a natural death. It didn't; the old campaign started up again. Most of the guests harped on the oil for the range (the smallest expense of all, as a matter of fact), so, to make them happy, we installed a gas range with a quarter meter, which also controlled the hot-water tank.

This pleased everyone, but the requests to be charged continued and at last they wore us down; Fred had a new invitation printed which said that anyone who cared to could contribute twenty five cents a night; this would be used for barn upkeep.

It was astonishing how good this made everyone feel, and yet, in many cases, it had no meaning at all. For instance, often a person would come out on Saturday, and stay until Sunday evening which meant two trips for Fred, twenty-eight miles altogether, and more than an hour of Fred's time. This guest might take two or three showers, if it was hot weather, leaving the water running a little each time, although he had been told our well was low. He might let the electric light burn in the kitchen all night, break a dish or two, forget to empty his garbage, leave a pair of shoes behind which he would ask to have mailed to him, but he would figure that by gosh he had given us a quarter and we were square.

Of course I'm exaggerating; I'm quite sure no one person ever did all of those things in one overnight stay, but it was interesting to see that paying that twenty five cents a night seemed to make all the difference. When there was no charge, they probably felt they were sort of accepting charity, but if they paid something (even though not nearly enough to defray expenses) they had handed out the amount asked for a certain commodity; if it was a bargain, well, who doesn't love a bargain?

If you live in the country, are overrun with guests and are tempted to have a guest house at all similar to ours, you will find it has many advantages but will cost you money. Even if you should break down and let your friends pay a small amount, you will find it won't cover current expenses. We abandoned the practice of a charge some years ago; it was meaningless.

Then there's the question of that modern curse, liquor. I mean curse in the sense that many people are finding it a serious problem to try to serve as much liquor as custom demands and keep its cost from mounting to a ridiculous proportion compared, for instance, to the cost of their food.

With hospitality off the leash, and the place overflowing with your friends, even if they aren't house guests, you can imagine what happens to the liquor supply.

The serving of drinks is Fred's department, not mine; in fact, I seem to be deficient in various aspects of entertaining. For one thing I have never got used to the idea of having to scrabble around for something to serve people who are coming to see me for only an hour or so.

When someone is due for an afternoon call, Fred, who is conscious of what most people expect and who is also well-acquainted with my shortcomings, will ask me: "What are you going to give her?"

"Give her?" I repeat, blankly, trying to persuade myself he means: which—a head of lettuce from the garden or a bouquet of flowers?

"Sherry? Tea? Got any decent cookies?" he goes on, ruthlessly.

We're at lunch and he knows perfectly well we have no decent cookies or there would be some on the table instead of ginger snaps.

"Cookies? Well, no, not *cookies*," I answer, hoping to give the impression that I have an abundance of other decent things.

"Got a cake in the freezer?" he continues. (The most persistent creature in the world, once he starts to worry a bone.)

"Uh-h, er, no, not *cake*," and I take a big bite of sandwich which obviously prevents my saying anything further. With luck the telephone will ring and the subject will be dropped.

It *is* dropped, for Fred knows perfectly well that the seed he has so pitilessly sown will sprout, that I will tire out my brain (capable of much more interesting thoughts) concocting some totally unnecessary and not especially appetizing thing to serve with a hot drink, or sherry.

I feel it's preposterous for me to be expected to fuss around and serve food and drink in the middle of the afternoon when no one is hungry, and the illogical thing about that is that when I'm at a friend's for a short call, I find myself thinking: well, well, where's the hot coffee? A little coffee isn't much effort.

When my sister Elizabeth was here recently, I invited Mrs. Hevenor, an ex-patient of hers, to tea. I also asked a friend of mine, Betty Simonds, and the two women came together, bringing a third one, a house guest of Mrs. Hevenor's.

Nowadays, "tea" can mean anything from a hot drink up (or down) to cocktails, so it seemed a waste of motion to prepare any food in advance; the sort of thing that is nice with coffee or tea isn't always suitable for cocktails. Besides, what if I fell downstairs and the party was called off? All that work for nothing. Much better to wait for a last-minute inspiration.

After our guests had been here for about an hour, I involuntarily exclaimed: "Good heavens! I asked you for tea!"

Of course they all said not to bother, and of course I insisted on bothering, and asked them what they would like: tea, coffee, cocktails, sherry. And that was silly for of course they all said they didn't care.

A few minutes before this, there had been some comments about Mrs. Hevenor being outspoken, so I said to her: "Since you're a frank person, won't you please tell me what you would like?"

It was a July day but not at all hot; however, she replied: "Well, iced tea would be nice."

Now this happens to be something I never make, never drink, and on top of that, I have an aversion to fooling around with ice cubes. But let no one say that when pushed to the wall I don't come through as a perfect hostess. I was about to exclaim: "Fine! Does that suit everyone?" when Betty broke in:

"Iced tea? That's a horrible lot of work! Don't bother with *that*, Ruth. Are you sure you have some sherry?"

We did, and sherry it was for all of us, along with some delicious cheese crackers which Betty unearthed in the cupboard and which I didn't know we had. (I would like to add that Betty is a wonderful friend in other ways, too.)

I have wandered far afield. Back to our arithmetic: a guest house similar to ours may, if you can manage to get it onto a proper basis, save you wear and tear physically, nervously, and spiritually, but I don't see how it can fail to cost you money. As I said, we abandoned the twenty-five cents a night motif because it served no real purpose, and too, we had always disliked it. It did me a good turn, though: provided me with an anecdote (a slightly unbelievable one) with which to finish this chapter.

While the nightly charge was still in effect, Joe Coffey told us that he knew a man named John DeWolfe who wanted a cheap vacation; could he come to the barn?

DeWolfe came, settled in one of the bedrooms, and stayed three months. He made rather a nuisance of himself in quite a lot of small ways, and also did something which we were at a loss to understand at the time: he made trips to New York five or six times during the summer just for one night, but every single time he went, he put all his belongings into a carton and stowed them behind a screen in the barn livingroom.

It was true that people who had to leave but expected to come back at a later date might store some things, but since DeWolfe always returned the following day, we couldn't imagine what he thought he was accomplishing. We found out at the end of his stay. When he undertook to pay the twenty-five cents a night contribution, he deducted a quarter for each night he was in New York. And to make it legitimate, he had moved out of his room for those nights.

When Joe asked us how we had made out with him, Fred replied: "Not so good, Joe. I'm going to devote the rest of my life to keeping DeWolfe from de door."

(Yes, I know; I don't like a *calembour*, either, unless it's my own.)

CHAPTER XII

A War Casualty

THE WAR AND CONSEQUENT GAS RATIONING made a radical change in our guest situation, both in the house and barn. Almost overnight unexpected callers became extinct. Once when a car drove in I called out to Mary (who feels about as I do regarding unannounced visitors and who had been with us several weeks) and asked who it was and she replied: "You know very well it's either the milkman or laundryman. If this keeps up much longer, even *I* will be glad to see a strange car come in."

One day (this was in May 1943) we got a letter from a Mrs. Hoffman, who had heard about the barn, asking if a German refugee, whom she knew, could spend the summer at our place. His name was Fritz Max Cahèn, and she related the following: he had been of considerable importance in Germany both as an editorial writer and a political economist, and had been present at the signing of the Versailles Treaty as political advisor to his friend, Count Brockdorff-Rantzau, who represented Germany at that ill-starred conference.

From the time of Hitler's first appearance Cahèn had warned his countrymen against him; later he helped many of the Führer's intended victims escape into Czechoslovakia, over the little-known paths he had become familiar with on hunting trips in the dense mountain forests along the border.

When the Nazis eventually got after him (he is a Jew), he managed to escape via that same route, with his wife and sixteen-year-old son, and for a few years they lived in Paris where he worked as a foreign correspondent. But when the Germans advanced into France the Cahèns had to flee once more and were separated somehow, Cahèn himself eventually coming to

America. His wife and son got no farther than England where the boy was interned; Mrs. Cahèn, however, was left at liberty and after a time found a job.

In America Cahèn, through his influential connections, received much inside information which he used in a daily report on the radio at Greenwich, Conn. He also wrote a book: *Men Against Hitler*. Then America got into the war, and as a technical enemy alien, Cahèn lost his radio job. Always high-strung, the ensuing months of mental and economic strain proved too much for his equilibrium.

Mrs. Hoffman's letter went on to say that Cahèn had had a breakdown and was in an institution, but the doctors believed he might recover if he could go to a quiet place in the country and do some outdoor work. He had no money, but there was an organization which would be willing to pay for his food and other needs in case whatever work he was able to do didn't cover his expenses. However, Cahèn was not to know this; the doctors considered it important that he think he was supporting himself.

Mrs. Hoffman lived in Riverdale, and Fred telephoned her, saying that even if Cahèn was a first-class farm hand we didn't need him, and couldn't afford him, but he was welcome to come to the barn if someone would pay for his food and personal expenses. Mrs. Hoffman said these would be taken care of, and a friend of Cahèn's drove him out to our place a few days later.

He was a tall, distinguished-looking man, dignified, completely silent. A formal bow was all I got from him. Since his illness he had grown a beard, brown, well-kept, and this, we had gathered from Mrs. Hoffman, was supposed to be one of the indications of his mental illness. I was disinclined to accept that; I had never seen my father without a beard, and my brother Rex has worn one for about twenty years.

Cahèn was left in the livingroom while his friend and I went out in the yard for a few minutes; there were some things she had to tell me about him. We were sorry to do this; Cahèn must have known he was our topic of conversation, but it couldn't be helped.

I was told that he probably wouldn't talk at all; he had gone into the silence some months back and hadn't spoken to anyone since. His contention was, I believe, that no one had paid the slightest attention to him when he had had something really important to say—a warning against Hitler—so now he wasn't going to talk anymore about anything.

His friend also said that he might not do one stroke of work, but we mustn't worry about that. She said he was an excellent cook, and liked good food, and she was sure that if we kept the barn refrigerator well-stocked he wouldn't go hungry.

When she went in to tell him goodby he gave her a haughty nod of dismissal and she departed; I was alone with a very mixed-up man. (Fred was doing his "duty" in a war plant that year in Danbury and didn't get home until seven o'clock.) I had always been much more afraid (theoretically at least) of unbalanced people than was called for, but I now found, to my great surprise, that I wasn't a bit apprehensive.

About five minutes after his friend had left, Cahèn walked casually out to the kitchen where I was starting to prepare dinner and opened up a conversation. He talked intelligently and normally, and after the first few minutes I completely forgot that he wasn't supposed to be a normal man, and also forgot to be delighted that he had broken the long silence which had been of such concern to the doctors.

He had dinner with us that evening; I even remember what we had—lentils and sausage—and he seemed to enjoy it. He talked pleasantly, interestingly; there was nothing at all noticeably abnormal about him.

The next morning he asked me for a job. Our lawn needed mowing but could you tell a dignified, impressive-looking highbrow to go cut the grass? I found I couldn't, but I had to think up something for him to do, as at least a part of his cure was to create the illusion that he was earning his way.

I had reduced my garden to half-size a year or so before,

and had thus regretfully stopped caring for half of the asparagus bed; I showed Cahèn this abandoned section, telling him
I hadn't the time to keep it weeded, and I asked him if he'd
like to take it over.

He agreed, and an hour or so later looked me up to say
that in Europe they bleached asparagus and he would like to
turn that half of the bed into an European one. I was delighted,
knowing just enough about bleached asparagus to be sure that
he would be occupied for quite a while; it would be a long
time before he would be ready for another job. He immediately
began heaping dirt on his half of the bed.

Cahèn had lunch with me that first day. (Fred was bringing
his supplies out that evening.) He made an asparagus omelet
which was a great deal better than I would have supposed
either eggs or asparagus could possibly taste and I'm especially
fond of both.

The following Sunday I asked Fred to help me with some
small but intricate job in the yard and we were busy with it
when Cahèn appeared, carrying a shovel and rake.

"You're not going to work in the garden today, are you?"
said Fred. "We relax on Sunday .This is just a little project
that Ruth needed me for."

Cahèn smiled and replied: "I also have a project; I am
impatient to offer you some white asparagus."

A week later I wrote Dottie Hoffman, telling her all of the
above hopeful signs of Cahèn's recovery, and others too. She
telephoned me two days later to say she cried with joy as she
read my letter. At one time Cahèn had lived with Dottie and
Leo Hoffman; they were his closest friends in the United States.

Since this isn't a case history, I will tell only of those ab-
normalities of Cahèn's which made him in any way a problem
to us. He seemed almost normal for the first month or two,
then he stopped sending his clothes to the laundry, and for the
rest of his stay, about three months, he wore the same khaki shirt
day after day. We interfered with him almost not at all but
finally Mary tried to persuade him to let her wash the shirt.

He smiled in his courteous, tolerant way and replied: "No, thank you; I am intent on giving it a fine patina."

Although a wonderful cook and loving good food, he suddenly decided he was going to eat nothing but raw vegetables, and something in his tone when he told me this gave me the impression that he expected me to beg him not to, or rush to the telephone and call the Hoffmans. If he did, I disappointed him, for I said, even with enthusiasm:

"That's a good idea. It must be an awful bore to cook for one person." Then I added truthfully: "For an experiment I once ate only raw food for a year, and I was in New York at the time and couldn't get really fresh stuff, as you can here. If I didn't have to cook for someone else, I'd eat mostly raw food."

The next thing he decided to do was to sleep on the floor, and when he announced this, I said: "Scott Nearing preferably sleeps on a board. And I remember that my oldest sister, May, if she was especially tired during the day, would stretch out on the floor for a while; she insisted it was more restful than a bed."

Poor Cahèn, what could he do to startle us? Rex wore a beard, Scott slept on a board, I liked a raw-food diet, and one of our neighbors, who came in frequently, wore a shirt that was even dirtier than his. He now began to go barefooted, but surely couldn't have expected to get a rise out of us over that, for he had seen me do it out-of-doors every day.

Fred's opinion was that all of these things, except perhaps his laundry notions, had nothing to do with Cahèn's psychosis, but were neurotic attempts to gain attention.

It being a war year, there were very few other guests in the barn which was a blessing, for Cahèn began to be very untidy in the kitchen. It actually wasn't very dirty but cluttered beyond anything you could imagine, and whenever Elizabeth or Mary came out, they would try desperately to straighten it up. Cahèn loved to say to me reproachfully: "Your sisters make such disorderly order out of my orderly disorder."

Speaking of the girls coming out, I am saying very little about any of my family as guests, because I don't feel they are. When Juanita is expected for lunch, I never know what we are going to have until she arrives and the meal is brought in from her car. She's generous, a good cook, an able and willing worker; what lady of the house would interfere? Or want to?

When Mary is around, I am merely her assistant in the house-cleaning department; she takes the stand that at times a house requires more than a lick and a promise, while I contend that a promise, on top of a lick, is pure extravagance. Once when I felt we had done a thorough job and was mildly protesting at her added touches, she said: "Remember that when we were kids and you were getting ready for a party I liked to fuss with your sash and hair-ribbon? That's all I'm doing now: tying your sash."

And when Elizabeth comes, she goes over my clothes, doing a thorough job of mending, lengthening, shortening. She tells me what to wear when we go out to dinner, and what not to wear ever again.

As to the other side of the picture, well, I try to co-operate, and if staying out of the way while other people work is an asset, I don't do too badly.

Back to the problem at hand. October arrived, and since the barn had no heating facilities, the Hoffmans and we did everything imaginable to get some action out of the refugee organization which was paying Cahèn's expenses. We couldn't seem to get it across to them that time was of the essence: the barn was cold and very soon now the water would have to be turned off.

Cahèn wouldn't have consented to move into the house even if we had been courageous enough to ask him to; he had to have privacy, couldn't bear the sound of a radio, and so on. The Hoffmans sent a psychiatrist to talk to him, which didn't get anybody anywhere—except the psychiatrist, who got a very nice fee.

Finally Dottie located a private institution in New York State which she thought was ideal for several reasons. It was costly but the organization agreed to pay for it because there seemed to be hope of Cahèn's cure.

I have forgotten what started me to thinking that there might be some legal red tape involved and that we could get into trouble if we took Cahèn to this institution; I imagine my idea had something to do with taking him from one state to another. At any rate, since Fred was working at the factory all day and I couldn't drive, Mary would have to be the one to take him, in her car, although of course I would go too. I told Mary that I could be completely wrong but that I thought we might be arrested if we took Cahèn and I asked her if she was willing to risk this.

"Well, of course," she said, surprised at such a question. "It's certainly better for us to go to jail than for Cahèn to be put in a state insane asylum."

That seemed to be the alternative.

We undertook to get Cahèn to agree to go to the institution and, to our surprise, succeeded. It then developed that there was no vacant room; he would have to wait a week or two.

I was frantic at the thought of a delay. There was not any telling how Cahèn would feel later about going, and I wrote to the head of the institution and told him this. I said that if he himself had a son or brother who needed to enter his hospital immediately, he would somehow find a place for him. I put everything I had into that letter, and won. The man immediately telephoned us long distance and said to bring the patient at once.

Then what happened? Cahèn wouldn't budge.

So there was nothing left for us to do but to call in two doctors and have him committed to Fairfield State Hospital.

The most poignant thing I have ever seen was Cahèn walking sadly across the yard between two men who were holding tight to his arms. They didn't want to appear to be taking him forcibly but he insisted on this; he wouldn't put himself in the position of going willingly, of being a part of anything which to him was so outrageous.

It wouldn't be accurate to say that we had grown attached to each other, Cahèn and we, but there were tears in his eyes when he said goodby, and in mine too.

He was in the State Institution for ten years, a model inmate. Fred and I went to see him often, and his son came down a few times from Canada. Mrs. Cahèn was working in England; she and I corresponded through the years.

Three years ago, through the Consul and by his own efforts, Cahèn was released and sent back to Germany. He is there now, writing and supporting himself. His wife will join him shortly.

To me it would seem almost insulting to give Cahèn a fake name just because he was treated as if he was mentally ill. I can't see the disgrace, even if he had been, but actually he never belonged in an institution. He was without family, money, and later without a visa in a foreign country. Under these circumstances there was no other door open to him. While he was in the hospital he had freedom to go where he liked and was kept there only because nobody knew what else to do with him.

With the end of the war the barn had occupants again, but never as many as during the first years.

Arkady and Masha came back to America. They wanted very much to stay here, and got some work in New York addressing envelopes at home, which was one light-housekeeping room. Masha also found some sewing and knitting to do. But it became more and more of a struggle to get by on what they were able to earn, and one Monday morning Arkady telephoned to say they were going back to Paris; could we come in to say goodby?

Fred was unable to go just then; he was creating some fine things in wood, now, and had more orders than he could accept. I went in on the afternoon train, to find that Masha had just been asked to make another sweater and they had decided that perhaps they could make a go of it after all. I returned home.

The following Monday we went through the very same performance, except that this time Masha had been given an order for six pairs of socks and a woolen cap. It was pitiful that the margin of their staying or going was almost literally a matter of dimes.

When they telephoned again on the third Monday (I don't know why it was always Monday) Fred said: "They can't go on like this. They'll never swing it. We'll drive in and I'll kiss them goodby too, and when *I* say goodby, I mean it."

They sailed, and have never returned.

Less and less often nowadays, the barn is used by people who haven't much money to spend on a vacation; I hope this is because fewer people are broke.

There has been one new development in recent years which we find most pleasant. Now and then, especially on long holiday weekends, somebody will reserve the entire barn, bring some friends, and give what amounts to a delightful house party. Fred and I are included in all festivities and we find that being guests on our own premises is about as satisfactory a holiday as one could think up. In fact on these occasions we are inclined to feel that the barn has turned into a worthwhile racket.

When the telephone rings, if I could have my choice it would be Virginia saying she, Millard, Roger, Gerry and a few friends would like to come to the barn for the weekend. They don't bring children or dogs, but even if they did it wouldn't faze me.

Once, years ago, Millard did bring their boxer, and when I stepped out into the yard Sunday morning, Millard was sitting on the grass, his face buried in his hands.

"What's the matter?" I asked.

With his eyes still covered he replied: "I can't bear to watch while that blasted dog of ours romps in your flower beds."

One time, in April, Virginia and a friend, Patty Hastings, were coming out for a day or two as house guests; when the station wagon rolled in shortly before lunch, it didn't stop at the house, to dump the luggage, but went on to the parking lot just beyond the barn. I went out to greet them; Virginia's two boys, Chip and Bobby, were standing by the car.

"Ignore them," Virginia said. "Mother couldn't have them, after all, but they'll stay in the barn and "—she gave them a meaningful look—"we will hardly know they're in Connecticut."

I laughed, hugged the boys, then was suddenly startled to hear a yelp from the other side of the car. Walking around to investigate, I saw a dog tied to the wheel. Not a boxer this time, but a dog of any breed leaves me, to say the least, indifferent.

"We sort of hoped we could keep him a secret," said Virginia, wistfully. "The boys assured me that you and Fred needn't even know he was here."

I was about to say it was all right, that the flower beds hadn't been planted yet, when Patty handed Chip a bag and asked him to take it to the house. The boy's eyes opened wide.

"But I'm not allowed in the house," he said.

His mother told him it was all right this once, and he trudged away.

"My heavens, Virginia," I protested, "you must have made regular ogres out of Fred and me."

She waved a hand. "I impressed it on them," she said. "Now they'll dash in only twenty times an hour instead of a hundred."

That just about brings the barn history up to date; I'm not pretending I've covered it adequately. A few years ago Fred and I tried to count the number of people who had used the barn and we remembered six hundred (not all by name, of course). There were no doubt scores of passing strangers whom we had entirely forgotten. More than half of these six hundred were people we hadn't met until they arrived to spend anywhere from a night to a season.

The barn has cost us money but we think it's been worth it.

Also, we've probably come out on the short end as far as the saving of labor and time is concerned, but I can think of any number of things more worth worrying about than that.

Has the barn project accomplished anything? Has it been of any value to the people who have taken advantage of it? Well, you answer that question for yourself.

What has it done for us? Many things, but I'll mention only the most important: the invaluable opportunity it has given us to share. I don't mean this in any lofty sense, but there is a need in most people for a kindred spirit to mourn with them, or to rejoice with them.

When the mountain pink spreads its great splash of color on the plot where our mail box stands, it adds to our pleasure when cars stop to enjoy it. If my kitten has died, I want to tell someone who also loves kittens.

Through the years the barn has supplied us with a host of people who could share our pleasure in each new phase of spring, summer, fall. From lilacs in May to autumn leaves.

The country is full of gifts which we who become used to them sometimes forget to appreciate. When Mary arrives from New York, she always stands for a moment after getting out of the car and breathes deeply of the fresh pure air, and I feel like apologizing to it because I've casually been taking it for granted. If it's July, Leo Hoffman's first question is: "Are the blueberries ripe?" and I'm ashamed because I don't know. Elizabeth always comes back from a walk with a beautiful bouquet of wild flowers while I've been too occupied with the flowers I planted to give proper attention to those that have done very well without me. Stella Rivkin, walking down our road, saw the spring sun conquering the winter snow and ice and came back to the house and wrote a charming poem about it, and I had been growling because the ground wasn't thawing fast enough to suit me.

Yes, the country is up to the brim and even running over with beauty, delight, miracles, and we who live in it are inclined to believe we get something from it which no visitor

from the city possibly could. Perhaps we're right, yet many
city dwellers who have visited us have unconsciously opened my
eyes to something new (or old) which I, so used to it, so near
to it, am passing by.

CHAPTER XIII

Everyone Loves Dogs and Children— Yeah?

THERE IS NOTHING more natural, it seems to me, than to look upon Saturday and Sunday as an opportunity to enjoy ourselves, and to many of us that means spending some time with our friends. This often results in eating with them, which is a jolly arrangement for everyone but the cook.

Until I was married I had an office job of some sort during all of my adult life, and in those days the hours in most places were from 8:30 A.M. to 6 P.M., six days a week. So, although I can't remember ever disliking my work, my one free day was extremely precious to me.

One Sunday afternoon I was reading *The Brothers Karamazov* for the first time and would have been completely happy except that the time passed disgustingly rapidly. As evening approached I kept glancing at the clock so often that finally someone asked me what was the idea and I replied with a deep sigh: "My Sunday is almost over."

"So is everyone's," said Rex coldbloodedly, and returned to Macaulay, *his* then current love.

By the time I was married many working people had Saturday off as well as Sunday, so imagine my chagrin when I realized that although I had been cooking all week, I had to keep on with it during the weekend when most people were enjoying a change. Not only that: Sunday dinner is traditionally supposed to be relatively outstanding, and even Saturday's shouldn't be a leftover job.

Add to this the fact that those two days were supposed to be the ideal time to ask friends to dinner, and then consider the weekend guest fad! I don't know why I didn't just get a divorce; maybe I did ask for one and maybe Fred told me I was being unreasonable.

If we had been living in town there might have been some kind of a showdown regarding this, but problems and pains are lined with silver where birds sing and flowers bloom and the snow is white instead of grey.

However, it took me a few years to accept the situation with equanimity, if not with enthusiasm, and even though I soon became expert at thinking up easy Sunday meals, the idea itself continued to offend me. To make it even more repugnant, everyone else was sitting around saying interesting things (that I was too busy to listen to), or taking a walk to work up an appetite.

I would think wistfully of the arrangement we had at home in New York: Saturdays the icebox was filled with plenty of food of various kinds and on Sunday everyone was on his own. We weren't allowed to exploit each other, either, and anyone caught waiting on anyone else had to pay a worthwhile fine. You were, however, permitted to hire someone to, say, pour you a glass of milk, but service came high and unless you felt completely exhausted and/or very rich you poured your own.

With enthusiasm and with guile I told Fred all about this system and although he seemed to find it very interesting, he didn't grasp the underlying significance of it.

I don't believe I minded the actual work (or any other work I've ever had to do, for that matter) at all. My feeling about this was, I think, caused primarily by a sense of justice, not only in my behalf but in that of all the millions of other women who were in this identical fix and whose husbands probably expected much more in the way of a meal than mine did.

Of course I'm not talking about those women who got pleasure and satisfaction out of preparing and serving an elaborate meal, even on Sunday. Let them enjoy themselves by all means. They are lucky, too, in that, unlike the poet and the painter, they meet their public the moment the work of art is completed.

Fortunately for both of us, Fred expected very little in those early days before I woke up to the fact that there was nothing against trying to make food really palatable as long as you had to cook anyway.

It has been a long time since I've felt it's an imposition to have to cook on Sunday; resentment is a big waste of time unless you can eliminate the thing you are resenting. I wasn't getting anywhere at all with mine so, somewhat of an extremist, I decided to learn to prefer Sunday cooking to any other. I can't claim, and stick to the truth, that I have succeeded in this, but I no longer mind it.

One of the many contests I wouldn't dream of entering with any hope of winning is that of capable hostess, but I do have one asset in that field: a good memory of what my friends like in the way of food. Of course I know that's not an unusual talent; many women share it with me.

The serving of drinks is a separate department in most households and seems to be the man's job; I am sorry to say that in my limited observation many of them make a botch of it.

Fred's system is, I think, good: he mixes eight gallons each of Daiquiris and Manhattans and a couple of gallons of Whiskey Sours at one time and always has a half-gallon of each in the refrigerator. The mixing takes about three hours and the drinks last for some time, for we don't enjoy people who are hard drinkers and there aren't any among our friends.

With this preparation in advance, Fred doesn't have to spend a lot of time over drinks after guests arrive. He says to them: "There are Manhattans, Daiquiris, Whiskey Sours mixed and ready; I also have sherry, straight rye, a rum highball. What'll it be?" This way a person knows the score—what he can and can't have.

Most men I know aren't nearly as open and above board as this, although it's no doubt true that if I was more catholic in my tastes I might never have become so aware of their

rather confusing attitude when they offer you a drink. I learned
to drink after I was married, doing it if not the hard way, at
least the slow way, starting with tomato juice when others had
cocktails, then gradually working up through Dubonnet and
sherry to Daiquiris.

Having attained this height, I was proud, when my host
asked me what I wanted, to answer: "A Daiquiri, please." But
I was constantly running into a snag: if he had rum, he had no
limes or lemons or vice versa. So, rather early in the game I
learned to say: "Whatever you have," for before long I was
a veteran and could swallow almost anything. If it was *too*
dreadful I could sneak it to Fred, or boldly leave it in the glass.

Very often when I said "Whatever you have," my host
would reply: "Oh I have everything," so I would say: "A
Daiquiri, then," and much oftener than not he couldn't produce one.

Next I tried this: when asked what I wanted I would say:
"What have you got?" (Making it easy for him.) He would
reply: "Anything you want." (I should have known.) So then
I would say: "A Daiquiri, please." Well, he just didn't happen
to have any rum.

Why don't I now give up and ask for what someone else
has chosen with success? For three reasons: one, I am a con-
firmed believer in the integrity of my fellow man and when
a person tells me he has everything, I believe him; two, many
of our closest friends are young and when we're with them,
I'm the only one present with white hair so am asked first
about a drink; three, I am an incurable optimist and in spite
of all I've gone through, I invariably think: this time I'll really
get a Daiquiri.

The truth of the matter is that I don't give a darn about a
drink, or ever feel the need of one. Just being with people
stimulates me, and when others are drinking to pep themselves
up, I would be better off if I took some phenobarbital. Once
when everyone at a party was drinking beer and I was feeling

quite high from mine, I was startled when I suddenly realized I hadn't had any.

Not that anyone cares but just because they are so outstanding, I want to call the honor roll: the men who automatically produce a Daiquiri for me—Bob Allen, Pierre Lutz, Gordon Page, François Tufferd and Truman Young. Two of the five are Frenchmen; does that offer any clue toward an explanation of this fascinating problem?

If you don't like dogs your character will bear looking into, but if you don't "love children," it's a waste of time to look into it; it must be quite unspeakable. That is a common, if unvoiced, attitude and in my opinion it is born of careless thinking.

There are people who automatcally love all children; this is supposed to be a virtue and possibly is one. There are people who love certain children and are indifferent to all others. And I suppose there are people who can't stand children in general.

To my mind the careless thinking comes in when we confuse a dislike of children with a lack of enthusiasm over having them around. It would be easy enough to write (and no doubt boring enough to read) several pages elaborating this theme but I am going to confine myself to this: in the last few weeks I have asked sixteen grandparents if they were glad or sorry when their beloved (and I mean beloved) grandchildren went home after a visit of more than a few hours and they all admitted they were glad.

If I couldn't stand children I might or might not have the courage to admit it. Since I don't at all dislike them but since I am about to say some unflattering things about them as guests, I thought it just as well to protect my reputation by explaining that I'm not at all against them as such, but that in my opinion adults and children don't mix well.

Whether you like it or not, though, there's no getting around it: a child sometimes enters your home as a guest. If he comes alone and you have a way with children, you both may enjoy it; if he comes with his mother and you have children of your own, it may even be a pleasure and an advantage to have him. In a childless home, however, you don't have to be a cranky antique to deplore this combination of guests—a child and his mother—particularly if you like his mother and would enjoy having a pleasant talk with her.

This is the situation from the child's point of view: he enters a room full of fascinating things, and if he's normal, he's curious and wants to handle and examine the unfamiliar objects. If he isn't allowed to empty the ash tray on the floor, tear a magazine, topple over a vase, he's naturally frustrated and unhappy; if he's allowed to do these things he's unjustly, although only momentarily, disliked.

The mother has no better bargain; most of them who are visiting with their small children sit on the edge of the chair, ready to pounce. They are unable to either talk or listen, and I have yet to see one who looked as if she was having a good time.

There are a few who keep up a nervous chatter, trying to ignore the destruction in progress around them, hoping to goodness you don't see the unusual things going on, praying that the book her child is tearing isn't an autographed first edition. This woman is trying to make the best of a bad situation, but the best isn't very good.

And what about you? Unless you're a sadist you're uncomfortable. And I'm not criticizing anyone. "Children will be children," whatever that means, and it's probably also true that mothers will be mothers. I've never been one and doubt if I'd be much good at it.

I know only one mother—Virginia—whose children do not touch other people's things. It seems like a miracle to me but Virginia says that if you start when they are very young you can, with time and patience, make it clear to children that they must never handle anything without permission except their own belongings. She believes that, aside from the more obvious advantages, it is pleasanter for the children not to handle a thing at all than to have something fascinating which they have just picked up taken away from them.

For a few years we had no prohibition against children in the barn but it didn't work out. If your own children waken you at dawn that's one thing, but when several groups of people were staying there and only one group had a child who woke up half a dozen innocent adults, it was hard on everybody, including the child.

In an environment where everything was strange, if the parents didn't watch the child every moment he could get into poison ivy, pick the flowers and vegetables and trample on the plants, turn the water on in the barn and leave it running, or fall in the pool. Luckily no child ever hurt himself badly on the tools in Fred's shop, and none ever drowned, but pulling youngsters out of the pool was almost routine.

Finally we sent out a revised invitation: no small children, no pets, no radio.

We like it, though, when older children come. A few summers ago, Roger's second daughter, Nona, asked to come out for a week with several of her girl friends; they were all around fourteen years old. Roger's older daughter, Linda, drove them out but she didn't stay.

The girls had the barn to themselves. The first night they played Canasta in the house with Fred until ten o'clock, then left, ostensibly to go to bed. But for the next two hours I heard constant screeches of laughter across the yard. My room is closer to the barn than Fred's, and I decided that if they hadn't kept him awake I wouldn't say anything to the girls; let them have fun, if that was fun.

The next morning they asked me if they had kept me awake and I said: "I couldn't get to sleep but I don't think it was because of the noise as much as the puzzle."

"What puzzle?" Nona asked.

"Well, I lay there," I replied, "and said to myself: they're not four-year-olds, they're fourteen. They don't laugh and then stop for a bit; it goes on and on like a whistle that gets stuck. I just couldn't figure out why the noise never stopped for a moment."

The girls gave each other sidelong glances, then one of them said: "It's just that we're so thrilled to get away from our mothers."

That really surprised me. I knew that Nona's mother, Gerry, was normally lenient, and had no doubt the other girls' mothers weren't tyrants. Besides, I had the idea that children had taken over of late years, that self-expression was rampant, and that it was the parents who were cowed. I didn't know what to conclude except that there must be something wrong with modern mothers if their fourteen-year-old daughters were so glad to escape from them.

I told that story to every mother I knew, pretending I was only relating an amusing anecdote, but hoping they would learn something from it if they could.

My young friends love to tease me about not liking children. Not long ago Bethany and Louise gave me a surprise birthday party at Bethany's, and a few minutes after I had arrived, Betsy said: "Do you realize what we've done for you?"

I glanced around. The dining table was loaded with tempting food but I knew that couldn't be what she meant.

"No children!" they cried.

Sure enough, not a little darling in sight, or even better, in hearing.

"Wonderful!" I exclaimed. "What did you do—drown 'em?"

"Parked all over Redding," replied Louise, "but they love you anyway," and she handed me a small box which contained a very pretty pair of earrings; the attached card read: "Happy Birthday from your Little Angels."

Dogs, when brought to our place as guests or even in their own environment, unless they are senile, exhausted, indifferent, are beyond my capacity for enjoyment. Puppies, excited, barking, are just barely tolerable if they don't like me, that is, if it is someone else's stocking they are chewing. If they do like me (and for some unaccountable reason most of them seem to) my evening as well as my clothes suffers damage, but like every other hypocrite I try not to let on.

The attention I care for least from a dog is a kiss on the mouth. We recently visited friends who proudly introduced their new puppy; it was one of those tiny things and as I stood looking down at it I was thinking: I'm relatively safe from you until I sit down. Now you will hardly believe this, but as I stood there feeling secure and pretending to admire the little beast, it made a straight dive up in the air and gave me a wet kiss on the lips.

At a luncheon party I attended not long ago, the hostess had a puppy which seemed to like particularly two young women who were seated together on the couch. Halfheartedly the hostess would say "Give him a push" and they would answer (sort of desperately, I thought) : "He's awfully cute" or "He's not bothering me; I like dogs." But when the hostess left the room for a moment, the women's expressions changed, and with frantic little kicks and pushes they did their best to save their nylons.

The puppy, naturally, thought they were playing games with him and entered into the fun with zest. The hostess returned and offhandedly repeated: "Give him a push." One of the women murmured: "He's *awfully* cute."

If you are interested in the good opinion of your fellow beings, it is, I realize, a reckless thing to admit you don't like dogs, and if you add that you love cats (as I do) , you may as well give up.

I do want to say this in my defence: I have loved two or three dogs in my life, and as a matter of fact I don't dislike any of them. In general I wish them all the best; in particular I wish they would all migrate to California.

CHAPTER XIV

Some Famous People—Mrs. John Doe

FOR MY MONEY, dragging well-known people into a book in order to keep the reader from falling asleep doesn't necessarily do the trick. I have known many a John Doe who would make a more interesting story than most of the career people I have met. For one thing people who have made a name for themselves fall, in my limited observation, into the same dull pattern: they are so intent on hanging onto their fame, on making sure that everyone is aware of it, that at a social gathering they are likely to be tiresome. And, as Fred says, they know so many long words with which to bore you.

Joseph Wood Krutch, who is one of our oldest friends, is an exception. He has, in my opinion, more to boast about than any other American writer, but he has mercifully escaped the need to talk about himself. I don't feel that he consciously avoids this from intelligence and good taste (although he's generously endowed with both), and I don't believe his reticence comes from modesty, or from conceit at being such a big frog in such a big pond that he doesn't have to keep everyone reminded of it. I think he simply has no urge to advertise himself—a cut above many career people and the men who deal in coffee and tooth paste.

It was a sad day for us when Marcelle and Joe moved to Arizona a few years ago. It would be difficult to find two people as different from each other as they are, yet both with so much to contribute to an evening's enjoyment.

It's no secret that Joe can like a person very much, yet like his privacy more. His friends were always bemoaning the

difficulty they ran into when they wanted the Krutches to come
to dinner; Joe was almost always against it. We, with Marcelle's
help, weren't above using tricks sometimes to get him to come
to see us.

He has a lively interest in animals and came over one afternoon to see the catbird eat raisins out of our hands; another
day he and Marcelle sat on our livingroom couch for two hours
watching Fred and me take turns cajoling our pet skunk out
from under the radio. On both of these occasions they stayed to
dinner, which Joe seemed glad enough to do, once he had come.

Full of sparkle, Marcelle is an addition to any gathering.
I don't know anyone more tolerant of the frailties of her fellow
human beings, yet at the same time more discerning about
them. Being married to Joe, she, of course, knows the intelligentsia by heart. One evening she and I were discussing a
mutual acquaintance. (I'll call her Kate.) I said:

"I try never to carelessly use the word stupid in speaking of
anyone; in fact, I know only a very few people whom I consider
stupid. Kate is one of them."

"Well, she's an intellectual, you know," replied Marcelle.

I was astonished at this and about to protest when Joe
entered the room. I asked him what he thought of Kate and
he answered that he scarcely knew her.

"Marcelle calls her an intellectual," I said, "but to me she
doesn't seem at all bright, never grasps your meaning of anything, but talks glibly and superficially about every subject
under the sun."

"Oh well, then you and Marcelle agree perfectly. That is
precisely her description of an intellectual," answered Joe.

For his sake, I'm glad they live in Arizona; the desert suits
him. They used to go out there for vacations before they went
to stay, and once Marcelle said to us:

"I wish you could see Joe in the desert; he's a different
person."

Possibly both Fred and I were about to say "That's fine,"

when Joe cut in: "I don't know that I like it when Marcelle tells people I'm a different person in Arizona and they all exclaim: 'Isn't that splendid!' "

Scott Nearing (whom, you may remember, Mother treated so casually at the very height of his fame) is another of our friends who doesn't feel the necessity for keeping everyone reminded of his achievements.

Some people with unusually strong personalities somehow make everyone present aware of them the moment they enter a room. This is done unconsciously, I believe, and not necessarily with bluster of any kind. They need scarcely make a sound, yet everyone feels their presence.

Then there are others having personalities equally as strong who can sit through an evening among a group of people with no one unduly conscious of them. You will, if you come to know them, be often impressed by their inner power, but a good deal of the time it will not be noticeable. Scott and Joe Krutch and Mother belong to this second group.

I have often wondered wherein the difference between these two kinds of personalities lies. It is a subtle thing and I don't believe it has anything to do with animal magnetism on the one hand or extreme modesty on the other.

A possible solution has just come to my mind; I may abandon it before I finish the paragraph. I wonder if it could be that Type Number One is the bossy person, either in a nice and helpful, or not so nice, way, according to how tactful and intelligent he is. When I think of the relatively few people I know in both categories, this answer seems to fit, but I'm not insisting on it.

If you met Scott casually you might very well get the impression that he was just an average, pleasant fellow with nothing special to offer, but if ever you were lucky enough to hear him give a lecture you would never forget it.

Once many years ago when he came back from abroad I met him at the boat. It was late at night, mid-winter, stormy.

Scott travels very light; his whole luggage was a large duffel bag. The weary customs man, who evidently hadn't even glanced at the owner of the bag, leaned over to open it.

"Here, it's tricky. Shall I do it for you?" Scott asked.

He has a rich, beautifully modulated voice and the man, recognizing it, glanced up swiftly. "Scott Nearing!" he exclaimed. Obviously he was an admirer of Scott's and as I remember it, okayed the bag without inspecting it, taking Scott's word for it that there was nothing to declare.

I think the incident rather pleased Scott. However, he always avoided any fuss about himself as a personage. Once, on the way from New York to his home in Vermont in a wind storm he and several other cars full of travelers were stopped by a huge tree which had fallen across the road. They all spent the night in a large nearby farm house.

They didn't bother to exchange names much that night, but after breakfast the next morning one of the men, who had taken a liking to Scott, said to him as they shook hands in farewell: "My name is Bill Smith. Yours is—?"

"Nearing," replied Scott briskly.

"Oh, Nearing. I don't suppose you're any relation to Scott Nearing?"

"Never heard of him," was the answer, even more briskly.

Of course it wasn't Scott who told me this; it was his travelling companion.

Through almost forty years of friendship, Scott insulted me only once as far as I can remember. After one of his visits with us he sent me a gift—a cookbook—and the name of it was *Let's Cook It Right*.

While I'm at it I'll present still another well-known person. Ed Nugent, an actor, and his wife, Suzanne, live here in Redding; Suzanne is an admirer of Fred's woodcraft and one morning some years ago she telephoned to say she had a friend visiting her from Hollywood who would like to see Fred's work. Could they come over?

When I opened the door to them a half hour later, Suzanne said, in her casual way: "Hi, Ruth. This is Joan Blondell."

Although I was expecting someone in pictures, I wasn't prepared for anyone quite so famous, and, too, this girl looked so young and unpretentious that I blurted out in my subtle tactful way: "Are you *the* Joan Blondell?"

She laughed and said: "Well, I'm *a* Joan Blondell. I don't know of any other."

I took the girls over to the shop, left them with Fred, and hurried over to the cottage. I knew Mary would be interested to hear about Joan; I had heard her say how much she liked her.

Excited at my news, Mary said she would hurry and change and come over but I told her she looked all right (she had on a neat house dress) and that Suzanne had said they had only a short time to stay. Mary said she couldn't come as she was; she would just skip it.

I went back across the yard to the house. A moment later Suzanne and Joan returned from the shop and had no more than entered the livingroom when Mary appeared; I introduced her and she said to Joan: "I've been in your cheering section a long time, and couldn't resist a chance to meet you. Please ignore my appearance . . ."

With a quick gesture Joan threw open her sport coat, revealing an attractive blouse and black satin slacks.

"See the way *I'm* dressed," she said.

The nice part of that was that she obviously meant it just the way she said it: Here we are, both dressed informally and who cares?

Then she and Mary, interested in the same people and the same world, if not both of it, sat down on the couch (Joan had been standing, ready to leave) and for half an hour carried on a lively discussion of the theater, pictures, personalities. Each recognized a kindred soul.

And now an incident about Mrs. John Doe. The thermometer liked to go down to thirty below now and then during our first years on the farm and I had to dress almost as warmly as when I was in Russia. Finding that the woolen stockings and socks I bought in stores didn't last worth a cent, let alone the high price I paid for them, I began to buy them from a man who came to the door selling woolen things which he made on a small knitting machine at his home. They were good-looking and durable.

One day he brought his wife with him when delivering my order which contained, along with some tan stockings, gay blue-green and rose-colored socks. The woman burst out with: "You wear awfully bright colors for an old lady, don't you?"

That startled me. For although my hair was quite white, I wasn't fifty yet and hadn't planned on thinking of myself as old for another thirty years or so. As I remember it, I answered meekly: "Well, yes, I do."

Our guests, at first surreptitiously and then more and more openly, admired the various and somewhat unusual things in our livingroom, such as the samovar and the old brass Sabbath lamp hanging from the ceiling. We carried on what must have been a quite innocuous, if not anemic, conversation.

Finally they rose to go, but just outside the kitchen door, the woman stopped and asked what on earth *that* was. "That" was a miniature colonial house built under the kitchen window to protect from winter winds the two swinging doors of the house which Smoky, our cat, used for going in and out of the kitchen. There was a window with tiny curtains, and on the window sill a tiny flower pot with sedum in it. Smoky even had a wee mail-box with his name and a red flag on it.

Fred explained about the house to our caller. She heaved a deep sigh, turned to me and exclaimed: "Well! I've had the time of my life! Your place is a curio and so are you!"

Erle Stanley Gardner once called me a "character" and I didn't like it. I'm sure you don't give a darn whether or not I am both a character and a curio but I care, so why I tell that story, I can't imagine.

On the coffee table in our livingroom lies a green leather book, with *Guests* in gold letters on the outside cover. There are over eight hundred names in it, and since my theme is guests, it would seem almost secretive not to give these visitors at least a brief paragraph or two.

Over a year ago I wrote a book on my revolutionary method of gardening, and as the keynote of it is the saving of labor, it isn't surprising that it has brought me hundreds of letters and many callers. At a rough guess at least ninety per cent of the latter drop in without letting me know, so if any of you have been annoyed at my attitude toward unexpected guests, you can now enjoy yourselves. Think of me constantly having to drop whatever I'm involved in, including eating and taking a much-needed nap, to go out and show off a garden which isn't always worth showing off. One day, I remember, I was about to take a bath at ten A.M.; I finally accomplished it at six P.M. Once I'm in the tub, they just have to wait.

I'm somewhat aghast when visitors come from as far away as Pennsylvania, Rhode Island, New Jersey without first getting in touch with me. The worst in that respect was Ling Po who made a special trip from the Frank Lloyd Wright Foundation in Wisconsin to see my gardening method and didn't communicate with me until he reached New York.

Of course people can inspect the garden whether I'm at home or not, but most of them arrive with a long list of questions either on paper or in their heads. However thriving my crops are, however rich the dirt under the mulch, however many earthworms are wriggling about doing their job, none of those can answer the endless questions. Which isn't to say that I can answer them all either.

A lover who goes on and on about his sweetheart's charms, or a friend who insists on listing all of the excellent qualities of someone he admires, can be extremely unentertaining. In the past ten years we have made quite a number of friends here in Redding, most of them young enough to be our children, and

I could bore you for pages, if you weren't smart enough to skip, telling how much we like each one of them. They certainly belong in this book, for both as hosts and guests they add a good deal to our enjoyment of life.

They treat us as contemporaries except that they come to us for advice, sometimes in matters serious enough to affect their whole lives. We tell them what we think is best to do, not worrying about the responsibility; for one thing, you can do just as much damage in refusing to give an opinion as in giving it, and for another, we find that in vital matters people ignore advice unless it coincides with what they would do anyway.

I believe that so far these young people ask us to go to see them because they want us. When we begin to totter and are no longer an asset, I hope we will be sensitive enough to know it and sensible enough to stay at home.

CHAPTER XV

It's a Gift

So MANY THINGS have been said and written in recent years about the roles of host and guest that it seems to me we have all become unduly selfconscious. There was a time when we gave little thought as to whether we would behave to suit our hostess when we visited, for we didn't, when we crossed a threshold, suddenly become some new species called "A Guest." We were still just ourselves, visiting a friend. No new role to play, no special rules to follow.

For those of you who were born in this acute host-guest era, I would like to be able to give my opinion as to whether or not the hostess suffered unduly, in the good old days, from the failure of the guest to realize that he had a highly specialized job to perform. But I have no opinion because I was blissfully unaware of the fact that my hostess and I were doing some kind of a stunt which required a great deal of skill.

Actually it takes more than skill; it takes genius always to be a perfect guest. For what one host likes in his visitors, another may deplore. We need a separate set of rules of behavior for each home in which we spend a weekend. Friends are not going to supply us with these rules, for most hostesses are hypocrites, in a nice way, and whatever you do to upset their schedule or plans, they will pretend that it is perfectly all right. *They* know *their* role: the guest can do no wrong, and although you may drive them crazy, accomplished hostesses will never let on.

That is why I say you have to be a genius, or at least must have a special sensitivity which warns you that you are stepping out of line.

Many questions go through your mind: what time do you

get up? Do you strip your bed the day you leave? Do you help your hostess or would she rather you stayed out of the way? If the radio is going while you are trying to talk, and no one is listening to it, and surely they have forgotten that it is blaring away, do you dare suggest that perhaps it would be just as well to turn it off? Do you let the dog wreck you entirely or do you (considering that you have the whole weekend ahead of you, to either suffer or take a stand) give him a few worthwhile pushes? If your hostess keeps picking on her husband, or vice versa, do you pretend you're deaf, or do you try to come up with some gay remark designed to smooth the ruffled waters?

And what about the weekend gift? If your friends have money, and it is practically impossible to think of anything to take them which they might want, let alone need, do you buy them a mere token of a present and let it go at that? Or do you spend three times as much as you can afford to show them that at least you are no cheapskate?

If your friends are poor, do you take them something beyond your means, but very welcome? Or do you realize that that might put them in a position of spending more than they can afford when they visit you? Perhaps you will settle for a trifle so that they may feel free to do the same. But, in any case, whether you think it is an undesirable custom or not, you will take a weekend gift unless you are a rebel in a big way.

I think that among the many minor things which make life pleasant, there are few that rate more highly than receiving an unexpected gift. During that minute you are unwrapping it, it could be any number of wonderful things: a dainty, luxurious garment, or the perfume you prize but can't afford, or some persimmons which you almost never see at the local market.

When the knot is difficult to untie, it is all the better, for the anticipation is prolonged; I wouldn't cut it for anything, and am sure some people have me down as a petty ribbon-saver. Finally I get it opened, and even if the gift turns out to be something I neither need nor want, it's enough that my friend felt the urge to send it.

On the other hand the weekend present had better be good in its own right, for it is totally lacking in spontaneity. You aren't receiving it because someone wanted to give it, but because he felt he should, so if the gift itself has no value for you, you are left with nothing. And if the one who gave it couldn't quite afford it, you have worse than nothing: the painful consciousness that your friend has spent money on you which he could have well used for something with some meaning for himself or someone else.

There are, of course, people who love to give presents even when custom forces them into it, and whether or not they can afford to. Then, even if the gift as such is a complete failure it isn't a total loss, for the donor enjoys making the gesture, and no dollar is thrown away if someone gets pleasure out of the way it's spent.

If anyone wants to take exception to that last statement, I hope he will notice that I said "thrown away" and not "misspent." I suppose a dollar used to get drunk on, or to buy poison to kill somebody, might be called misspent but surely it isn't thrown away.

One of the complications connected with writing a book is that after you've said just about everything you can think of on the particular topic you've chosen, your manuscript may be too short to tempt a publisher. That's the sweet fix I find myself in at this moment.

It's true that this would already be plenty long,—in fact, too long,—if the person who edits and types my things didn't have a mania for throwing whole chapters into the wastebasket. She will listen patiently while I explain that those particular pages are necessary, expertly done, and really the making of the book, but in her quiet way she's adamant and a chapter once suspect is nine-tenths doomed. Perhaps this is as good a place as any to thank her for her firmness. She wishes to remain anonymous but consents to my putting in this one little clue: she has a hankering for tying sashes.

This problem of length is, however, mine, not yours. Whether I like it or not, I have to think up something more to say, which you lucky people can skip.

I don't need anyone to tell me that a book based on fact and told in the first person can get more and more tiresome the farther you go. Those obnoxious pronouns—I, me, and my—appear on every page and there's no way to avoid them.

Have you ever noticed how authors (especially female ones) of such books turn themselves inside out in an effort to be modest, to keep from boasting and pushing themselves forward? Then they get panicky: what if the reader should begin to feel that they really aren't up to much? So, in self-defense, various characters must make remarks about the author's brains, charm, accomplishments. I know I must have sinned in this respect, but, thanks to my editor, I think most of it is in the wastebasket.

Now, to humor the publisher, even though we are all somewhat fed up with pronouns in the first person, I'm going to talk about myself as both a guest and hostess. If I stop to ask myself which of these roles I prefer, I believe I would choose the latter. As a guest the uppermost thought is, roughly: I'd better behave so they will ask me again. As hostess: she had better behave if she wants to come back. Yes, I think I'd rather be hostess.

Going back to my childhood (when, of course, I didn't think of myself as either guest or host) I remember one grave fault I had: no matter who came to visit, even my own chums, I ignored the company if there was a new book in the house or if a copy of *The Youth's Companion* had just come; I got caught up with my reading. And when visiting anyone, I made straight for the bookcase. My best friend, Ethel Chapman, learned to hide all tempting reading matter when I was expected.

In my late teens and through my twenties I loved to give parties, abetted by Rex, Mary and Elizabeth. These were, actually, features of a highly original and sensational nature and I would like to describe a few dozen of them; I have a suspicion, though, that they wouldn't hold up on paper.

During the next twenty years there came a strange development which I can't account for. I imagine the psychologists would pounce on it and call it an escape. It was that I simply couldn't seem to stay awake.

This began when I had the Village tearoom, and it was understandable then, for I was always short of sleep. A young man (I've forgotten his name) came into the Klicket a few times, then asked if he could come to see me at home. That was a problem, for every afternoon and evening I was in the tearoom, and the morning didn't seem suitable.

I told Joe Coffey about this and he said he would pinch hit for me in the tearoom, so a date was fixed and the young man called. He hadn't much more than rung the doorbell when I realized that, nothing to do about it, I was due to fall asleep any minute. In desperation I suggested that we take a stroll in the moonlight; he looked at me in some surprise, then pointed out that it was pouring rain.

We sat down, I began to nod, jumped up and went to the kitchen and made a pitcher of lemonade. I put lots of ice in it, because I hate cold drinks and I thought the series of shocks as I drank glass after glass would save the situation.

It didn't. Once I sat down again in the livingroom I was lost. The next thing I knew my suitor was shaking me and saying coldly: "I think you had better go to bed. Good night."

I never saw him again.

When Fred and I decided to stop hoping we could ever get married, a number of my friends were intent on finding someone else for me to fall in love with. I wasn't interested but was co-operative up to a point and when Tabby asked Jack Sinclair and me to dinner, I obligingly went. Jack, a big pleasant Texan, had paid enough attention to me to put the idea into Tabby's head.

I arrived an hour or so before dinnertime and promptly went to sleep. That was all right in itself, but Tabby, knowing my failing, woke me up after a while and made me dash cold water on my face several times. Then her son came home and I fell asleep as he and I sat talking. Tabby shook me, saying firmly: "You've got to go home before Jack gets here. He would be so offended if you just sit and sleep that he would never want to see you again."

Being too far gone to argue, or care, I started home. Before I had gone a block I went sound asleep and fell down. A policeman helped me up and asked if I was sick and I said no, that I was just sleepy. I wonder why he thought it was all right to leave me at large.

After my marriage, at forty-five, I was still addicted to sleep; it was routine for me to take a nap when Fred and I were visiting, or had guests. Our friends got used to it and simply ignored it. Sometimes when we had weekend guests, I would sleep soundly in my chair for an hour or two during the evening, then wake up, ready for a good time, when every one else was about to go to bed.

One of the least appropriate times for such informality was when we had dinner here in Redding at the home of extremely conventional people whom we didn't know very well. After an elaborate meal served by a butler, I settled down in a big comfortable chair in front of a glowing fire and dozed happily until time to go. I didn't apologize for my behavior because I didn't quite know what to say. Surprisingly enough my hostess and I became good friends.

A year or so after that, without any reason at all that I know of, I abandoned that idiosyncrasy, about which I have a hazy theory: I have always been a small eater and a big sleeper; is it true, perhaps, that eating and sleeping pinch hit for each other if there is occasion for it?

I do know this: during that period I was quite helpless when sleep crept up on me. Nothing, I believe, except violence of some kind could have kept me awake, and ever since then I have felt that it is a completely unfair thing to shoot a soldier for falling asleep at his post; he is probably quite unable to help it. During those sleepy years of mine, I feel sure that no mere threat of being shot could have kept me awake. It might even have sounded attractive: eternal sleep!

Another failing I have, which is regrettable under any circumstances is a profound disability for remembering names and faces. At random I will take this example: the young man seated next to me at a large luncheon party some time ago obviously knew me but I couldn't remember ever having seen him before in my life. I suffered through the meal, doing my best not to give myself away; no one relishes having made no impression whatever on you.

When lunch was over I pointed out the man to Kay Powell, who was there, and asked her to try to find out his name and if possible where he had met me. Before long she returned with this news: "You had dinner with him and Neil last night at Neil's apartment. Just you three."

Knowing me well, she made no further comment, and I didn't bother to explain that my mind had been completely occupied the evening before with a new world-shaking idea I had just thought of.

This deficiency of mine isn't comfortable; it isn't pleasant to hurt people's vanity, which you do, of course, when you don't recognize them. Fred, and those of my friends who are aware of this failing, often help me out by giving me a quick clue.

One of the biggest, or at any rate one of the most ridiculous, slips I ever made was at the final clambake. A day or so before, I was bemoaning the fact that there would be any number of people who would come whom I ought to be able to recognize and wouldn't.

"What's the difference?" said Fred. "No one will be the wiser. Since you're the hostess, you're supposed to greet everyone like a long-lost brother whether you recognize him or not."

So I stopped worrying.

The cars which came had to park down at the other end of our meadow and from there the guests walked back. When I saw anyone coming more or less from that direction I made a point of greeting him with a sort of vague enthusiasm, trying to show by my manner that if by chance I had, somewhere, sometime, already met him, I was delighted to see him *again*.

The difficulty was that it wasn't always easy to tell whether or not a person approaching from the general direction of the parked cars was just arriving or only seemed to be, so I got into trouble. When I cordially shook hands with one man, telling him I was so glad to see him, he grinned and said: "I'm glad to see you, too. Still as glad as I was the other three times today that you've shaken hands with me."

In the first years of our marriage, before a big freezer came into my life and changed my whole outlook as far as the culinary department of our home was concerned, it seemed to me an economy of time and perhaps of money to cook a good-sized roast or casserole and eat it every day until it was gone. I didn't particularly like sitting down to the same thing, but any compromise was better than standing for ages over something that was cooking, especially when what you were standing over wouldn't turn out to be a treat anyway.

Fred was an angel about eating leftovers, but I remember three remarks he made on the subject.

One day when we had soup for lunch, he began to sort of study his and I asked what was wrong. (It wasn't very good; I didn't know why.)

"Nothing. Just reminiscing," he said. With his spoon he began to sort out various particles in his plate. He went on: "Calendar soup—here's last Thursday, this is yesterday, and this must be a week ago Saturday."

I started to point out that I had heard the French made soup in a somewhat similar fashion but stopped myself in time; I didn't feel it would be good policy to mention French cooking just then.

One Sunday we had a leg of lamb and continued on with it for quite a while. Susan Townsend came to dinner and that night I made a curry of the leavings. She tasted it, then asked:

"What is this, Ruth?"

Before I had a chance to reply Fred spoke: "It was lamb when we bought it. It's mutton now."

Then at last came his remark which made me realize I must mend my ways. I don't remember what the dish was or how often we had faced it but Fred took one bite, glanced at me and pleasantly observed: "I know when I'm licked."

As a matter of fact, so did I. We left the table, Fred got the car and we went up to the East-West House and had an excellent dinner. The very next day I turned over a new leaf.

CHAPTER XVI

This I Believe

WHEN SOMEBODY KNOCKS and I open the door, my first words are "Come in," even if the caller is a youngster of forty, working his way through college. This all-inclusive hospitality dates back, I think, to the time I tried to sell books from door to door. I was sixteen, and I took on the job, not primarily because I wanted to earn some money, but because the agent who talked me into it looked like my brother Walt. Walt was away from home just then and homesick; I had the absurd feeling that he wanted me to sell books. At any rate I have never forgotten how it feels to have the person who answers my knock treat me like a leper.

But these people who enter your house on business—salesmen, the plumber, the laundryman—are not the visitors people mean when they say unpleasant or even bitter things about guests. They mean the relatives, friends, and acquaintances whom they deliberately invite, and, too, the ones who invite themselves.

Benjamin Franklin's famous remark is often quoted with relish: "Guests and fish stink after three days." The implication seems to be that if Franklin, a wise and kindly man, got fed up with guests, why shouldn't we all? And those of us who like to quote him usually have something colorful of our own to add, until guests have come to rank with mothers-in-law in the realm of wisecracks.

It may very well be that our unflattering remarks about visitors are nothing more than a habit; perhaps our feelings about them are much milder than our talk. But the *attitude* is widespread. In order to get their reaction, I have told a number

of people I was writing a book about guests, and their comments, although expressed in different words, were identical
in meaning: "What are you going to call it? Guests are pests?"

If entertaining is actually a problem, I believe that with rare
exceptions it is one that can be solved; I think it can be a
pleasure instead of a headache. However, no host is going to
solve it by attempting to make his guests behave differently.

First: did you ever try to change anyone, try to make him
act to suit your taste? Second: hardly any two people annoy
or disturb or offend you in the same way. So you have a Hercu-
lean task to perform if you're setting out to make everyone
who comes to see you behave the way you would like him to.
The solution, then, must be for the host to change himself, or,
rather, his attitude. If we hear someone complaining about his
guests, isn't it fair to wonder what's wrong with him as a host?

Visitors to our homes fall into several groups; I would like
to take these categories one by one and briefly try to figure out
where the trouble lies and how to handle it.

The man who has to be invited for business reasons can be
eliminated. "Business is business," we are told, and somehow
the inference seems to be that business is deplorable. Therefore,
if you suffer through a dinner with that kind of guest, I suppose
it's to be expected.

Then there's the relative from whom you hope to get something substantial when the will is read, so however hard he or
she may be to take, there is little to do, I should think, except
to try to earn your money without griping. This, too, in a way,
goes under the head of "business is business."

The relative who comes to stay with you permanently can
also be eliminated, for he becomes a member of the family,
and that is a different situation—or headache, if that is the way
you feel about it.

I will skip mothers-in-law. I never had to cope with one,
so am not qualified to give an opinion, let alone advice. However, if I was suddenly confronted with one, I think I would
try to treat her gently, kindly, but no nonsense.

Now comes Aunt Maggie, whom you were quite glad to see when she arrived. But you've had enough. Unfortunately, there doesn't seem to be a thoroughly pleasant, yet adequate, way of letting her know her time is up. It seems to me that if you're really fond of her, you can put your arms around her and tell her you love her but——. Take it from there.

If you actually don't like her much it's a different problem. Perhaps you let her stay, even though she gets on your nerves, because she's lonely and pathetic; your pity for her should see you through. If you keep your mind on trying to put a little joy into her life, you may be so pleased with your own virtue that you would be almost sorry to have her leave.

But if enduring her painlessly is beyond you, why don't you just tell her, subtly if possible, frankly if necessary, that it's time she went home? This isn't as brutal as it sounds; if you don't want her around, the chances are she's not very crazy about being there, and perhaps nothing but inertia is keeping her from moving on.

In my observation and experience many of the sacrifices we make in trying not to hurt another person's feelings are wasted. If there's friction and uncertainty in the air, the other usually feels it as much as you do, and suffers accordingly. The surgical approach is maybe the answer to more problems than we realize.

Then there's the lifelong friend, whom you had fun with when you were both young but who, unfortunately, has developed into a first-class bore. You feel you must ask him to your home now and then not only for old times' sake but because you do still like him and would rather suffer a little than hurt his feelings.

I find it relatively easy to protect myself from a bore. The pleasantest and simplest way is to turn the tables on him—*you* bore *him* for a change. Take over the conversation. If he outwits you, protect yourself by following your own train of thought: plan tomorrow's dinner, try to figure out a way to make the children obey you, worry about your income tax.

Or think of your good fortune: what if this dear old friend was going to stay two weeks instead of two days? What if he went into town on the same train you took every morning? What if you were married to him?

And now for unexpected guests (even though we've pretty well covered them already), the variety that arrives to give you a treat and stays all day. City dwellers love to drive to the country to some friends', and have a picnic. I won't generalize about these, but will tell of the experience of a neighbor of ours, whom I'll call Gladys.

Shopping is a problem for her and her husband. They have one car which he has to use to get to work, so on Saturdays they buy enough food to last all week. Then comes Sunday and a carload of unexpected visitors, bringing a lot of enthusiasm and a fine ham. The garden is full of vegetables, no problem there, but Gladys, who isn't young, has to cook enough for eight or ten people instead of two.

Worse than that, next week's supply of bread, butter, et cetera is consumed, and it's an effort, nuisance, and expense to replace them.

Unfortunately, Gladys couldn't quite get up the courage to be frank with her relatives and friends, so she began having Sunday dinner very early, before anyone showed up. This created a situation which called for discussion and explanation, and ended in mutual understanding and co-operation.

I can't help but think that our own way of handling this situation is the most satisfactory one. We simply tell everyone that we prefer to know it if they're planning to visit us, so we can be prepared. Or can tell them if it isn't convenient. I don't think we have lost one friend thereby, although it may well be that because of this attitude some of them have concluded we aren't all that could be desired. However, since as a matter of fact we aren't, they probably would have found it out anyway.

There are a few people who invite themselves to your home for a weekend, and they seem to do this oftener in summer than in winter; our barn takes care of that for us. But if someone does ask if he can come in the off season, we say no, if that's the way we feel about it. It's safe to be honest if there's mutual liking between friends; lacking that affection, what is there to lose?

The toughest cases are those married couples, one of whom you like immensely, the other a person to whom you aren't attuned. Who can say anything wise or helpful or even just not inane, about this situation? Each case is different in degree of pain and pleasure, each one is finally resolved on its merits and demerits. It's sad to have to give up a friend because he has married the wrong person (for you); on the other hand, just as it seems sensible to stop seeing some otherwise agreeable person who invariably gets drunk and ruins the party, so it may also seem wise to drop a friend who spoils the evening by bringing a husband (or wife) along.

Unless you're a genius at ignoring the bothersome trifles that confront us all a dozen times a day, any visitor may have annoying mannerisms or habits which get on your nerves. I often outwit this nuisance by playing a game with myself; this may be childish, but it works, so who cares?

For instance, we had a weekend guest last winter who passionately loved an open fire, so we had one. It turned out that she was addicted to poking it, and after an hour of this restless, far too frequent poking, I thought: I'll go crazy if she keeps that up for two days. But instead of going crazy, I made a game of it: I kept count of the number of times she poked, so that I would have a story to tell. Of course the more she poked, the bigger the story; I was disappointed each time she let several minutes go by without running up the score.

I doubt if there is any more difficult job in the world than living with other people, whether it's for a week, or for keeps. I am surprised, for instance, that any woman wants a maid who lives in, if she can possibly do her own work. It seems to me so much easier to clean a kitchen than to adjust to another personality.

I wish Benjamin Franklin hadn't used the word "stink"; I

don't like it. But since he did, I'll use it, too, this once; I'll put it in quotes, though, to show it isn't my choice. I don't believe it's the guests that "stink," I think it's the set-up, for three days spent in adjusting to company are three days of more or less strain. The difficulty lies in our own incapacity to live comfortably with outsiders making inroads on our time, our routine, our ability to give and take nonchalantly and pleasantly.

Allowing others freedom of movement and personality and at the same time retaining your own is perhaps more of a job over the short period of a weekend than for a longer stretch. There isn't enough time to adjust yourself to what they do or do not like: to be entertained, be let alone, take a nap, get up late (and hold up breakfast), get up early (and wake the household).

Most people want to be considerate, and this very wish is likely to make them nervous guests. They want to fit into the surroundings and do the right, that is, the thoughtful, thing. Even old friends, who have spent many weekends with you, aren't quite as easy in your home as they are in their own.

Along with all the complaints about guests being a trial, there's a good deal of discussion about what the host should do to make a visitor happy. Somebody once told me that it was essential to sleep in your guestroom a few times, to find out what was lacking. For me, that suggestion is worthless; all I need in a bedroom is a bed—hard, soft or medium.

This business of trying to please visitors, wholesale, is baffling; each has different needs. Henry hates a hard bed; Scott despises a soft one. Roger loves to linger for ages at the breakfast table; Janet likes to gulp down orange juice and coffee and get out into the country air.

You will of course remember some of these preferences, and do the best you can to humor everyone. But if, having as many guests as we do, you would try to cater to everybody's taste, you might get the feeling you are running a small hotel, or even a sanitarium. And end up by endorsing Benjamin Franklin and his followers.

I've finally come to the conclusion that the solution to this much-discussed problem is to pay scant attention to your guests' enjoyment and a great deal to your own. I believe that if you ask people to your home simply because you honestly want to see them, they will feel your mood and will relax and have a good time.

You may have to do a good many things, week in, week out, which you don't want to do. You may even be more than unusually unfortunate and not like anything you have to do. But unless you live with someone who loves to entertain and to go places and expects you to enter in, there are two things you can omit if you don't enjoy them: being a host and being a guest. Don't invite people to your home if you don't really wish to see them; don't visit them if it isn't a pleasure.

If there *is* such a thing as an acute guest problem, if all the talk about it isn't just talk, I firmly believe the answer to it, with rare exceptions, is surprisingly simple: invite people because you want to spend some time with them. The meal you serve may be a little less than outstanding, "gracious living" in the guise of fine linen and candles may be missing, the conversation may not once rise above the level of the commonplace, but if you're having a good time, I think your guests will too.

A happy host makes a happy guest. This I believe.

www.ingramcontent.com/pod-product-compliance
Lightning Source LLC
Chambersburg PA
CBHW021336090426
42742CB00008B/628